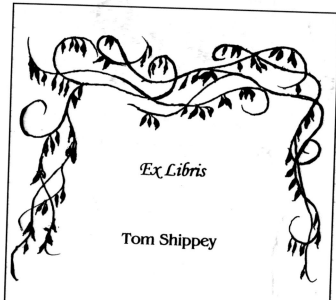

Joseph of Arimathie:

otherwise called

The Romance of the Seint Graal, or Holy Grail.

ISBN 0947992 81 2
Llanerch reprint 1992.

Joseph of Arimathie:

ÓTHERWISE CALLED

The Romance of the Seint Graal, or Holy Grail:

AN ALLITERATIVE POEM WRITTEN ABOUT A.D. 1350,
AND NOW FIRST PRINTED FROM THE UNIQUE COPY
IN THE VERNON MS. AT OXFORD.

WITH AN APPENDIX, CONTAINING
"THE LYFE OF JOSEPH OF ARMATHY," REPRINTED FROM THE
BLACK-LETTER COPY OF WYNKYN DE WORDE;
"DE SANCTO JOSEPH AB ARIMATHIA," FIRST PRINTED
BY PYNSON A.D. 1516;
AND "THE LYFE OF JOSEPH OF ARMATHIA,"
FIRST PRINTED BY PYNSON A.D. 1520.

EDITED, WITH NOTES AND GLOSSARIAL INDICES,
BY THE
REV. WALTER W. SKEAT, M.A.,

First published in 1871 by Trübner & Co.,
for the Early English Text Society.

LLANERCH PUBLISHERS
FELINFACH.

Also published or distributed by Llanerch:

WILLIAM OF MALMESBURY
ON THE ANTIQUITIES OF GLASTONBURY
translated by Frank Lomax.

THE ROMANCE AND PROPHECIES
OF THOMAS OF ERCELDOUNE
edited by James A. Murray.

TALIESIN POEMS
translated by Meirion Pennar.

SEVEN ANGLO-SAXON ELEGIES
FROM THE EXETER BOOK
translated by Louis Rodrigues.

A HISTORY OF THE KINGS OF ENGLAND
by Florence of Worcester.

For a complete list, write to Llanerch Publishers.
Felinfach. Lampeter, Dyfed. SA48 8PJ.

v

CONTENTS.

PREFACE.

§ 1. My object, in this preface, is to give first of all a general description of the four pieces which this volume contains, and afterwards to discuss briefly the legend to which they all refer. And it may here be observed that the first piece in the book, viz. the alliterative poem, is the one which, as being of some curiosity and importance as well as hitherto *utterly unknown*, the Early English Text Society chiefly desired to publish. The other three pieces are reprints from scarce books, appended to give the volume more completeness.

ACCOUNT OF THE ALLITERATIVE POEM.

§ 2. The alliterative poem here for the first time printed came under my notice when editing the A-text of Piers the Plowman from the celebrated Vernon MS.[1] At p. xvii. of my preface to the A-text, I have stated that a leaf has been cut out of the Vernon MS. just where Piers the Plowman ends, and where some other poem begins. The missing leaf is No. 402. Now, in Mr Halliwell's description of the Vernon MS., the piece next to Piers the Plowman is called "Judas," and it is said to begin on leaf 403; but "Judas" does not really begin till we come to the 2nd column of the back of leaf 404. The contents of leaf 403 and of part of leaf 404 are thus left unaccounted for; and, as a hasty glance at the MS. shewed that I had fortunately lighted upon some unique piece with which no one seemed to be acquainted, it was well worth while to

[1] For a description of this MS., see P. Plowman, A-text; pref. p. xv.

secure a copy of it; and an excellent transcript was accordingly
made by Mr George Parker, assistant in the Bodleian Library, from
which the copy now before the reader was printed, after careful re-
vision by myself. In the footnote to p. xvii of the preface to the
A-text of Piers the Plowman (already referred to) the *first* and *last*
lines were inadvertently given as the *two first* lines, and the word
nouwe was misprinted *nowe*.

§ 3. The poem being imperfect at the beginning, the next point
was to ascertain how much has been lost. This depends upon the
probable contents of the missing leaf preceding it in the Vernon MS.,
which again involves the question whether the Vernon MS. contained
the very rare twelfth Passus of the A-text of Piers the Plowman.
This twelfth Passus is indeed so rare that I have only been able to
find *one perfect* copy of it, viz. that in MS. Rawl. Poet. 137, which
was printed as a Supplement to the A-text, but issued to subscribers
with the B-text, as it was, unfortunately, not discovered till the
A-text copies had been issued. But the MS. in University College,
Oxford, preserves the beginning of this Passus,[1] and there are special
reasons why it is omitted in the Trinity MS. and in MS. Harl.
6041;[2] whilst of course it could not occur in MS. Harl. 875, the
MS. in Lincoln's Inn, or in MS. Dublin D. 4. 12,[3] which are all ex-
tremely imperfect at the end. The other MSS. of the A-text are not
of much account. Considering these things, and remembering the
extreme excellence of the Vernon MS., I think it almost certain that
it must have contained the *whole* of the A-text, the twelfth Passus
included. This would account for just exactly three columns of the
missing leaf; since, counting in the Latin lines, there are 135 lines
missing from the eleventh passus, and 102 from the twelfth, and the
title to the twelfth Passus would take up two lines more, giving 239
lines to fill up the 240 lines which three columns of the MS. con-
tain. At this rate, the number of lines lost at the beginning of the
piece now printed are as many as would fill a column. But as
"Joseph of Aramathie" is written out *like prose*, each column

---

[1] P. Plowman, A-text; note on p. 154.
[2] P. Plowman, A-text; preface, pp. xix, xx, xxi.
[3] Id. preface; pp. xvii, xxii. Also B-text; preface, p. vi, *note*.

averages about 96 or 97 lines; i. e. *rather less than a hundred lines are lost*. Finally, as the extant portion of the poem begins not very far from the probable beginning, I have little doubt that this result is sufficiently near for practical purposes; and, as nothing seems lost at the end (cf. note on p. 66), we have this result, viz. that our fragment contains the last 709 lines of an Early English Alliterative Poem which perhaps originally consisted of about 800 lines.

§ 4. I have said just above that the poem is written continuously, like prose. But that it is a genuine specimen of Alliterative verse was soon evident, and a little attention would soon have enabled me to divide it into lines of the right length. The scribe, however, has saved me the trouble, for he has marked off the whole poem into lines and half-lines (with tolerable correctness and only a few omissions) by the use of capital letters, paragraph-marks (¶), and metrical dots or periods; and I may observe that he clearly regarded the metre as consisting of *long* lines, not *short* ones.[1] The second column on leaf 403 begins, for instance, thus:—(ll. 102—105)—

Do a wei þi Maumetes. þei han trayed þe ofte. Let breken hē
a two . and bren hem al to pouder. Schaltou neuer gete grace.
þorwȝ none suche goddes. ¶ þēne seis þe kyng. my wit mai
&c, &c.

I have carefully observed, however, the scribe's use of capital letters, and the reader will find, accordingly, some few lines beginning with a small letter. He should notice, at the same time, how carefully the scribe has avoided using a capital in the middle of a line. The cutting up of the poem into lines is the only liberty I have taken, though of course I am also responsible for the punctuation, for the use of hyphens, and the expansions of the contractions; in all other respects the MS. is followed with scrupulous exactness. In the Glossarial Index, I have endeavoured to tabulate and explain every word which seemed worthy of note. Many of them, however, are more fully explained in Mr Morris's Glossary to his Early English Alliterative Poems, and in my Glossary to William of Palerne, to which the reader is referred.

§ 5. English poems in unrimed alliterative metre are compara-

---

[1] P. Plowman, A-text; pref. p. xxvii.

tively rare. I know of only about twenty-three, and have given a complete list of these in my Essay on Alliterative Poetry, prefixed to vol. iii. of Bishop Percy's Folio MS., edited by Hales and Furnivall. Our present poem is there numbered 21, and is very inadequately described, as I did not then know much about it, and made no attempt to assign to it its right place. But it ought, chronologically, to stand very high in the list, certainly not lower than *fifth*, and probably *third ;* this is what gives it its chief value. It is clearly one of the oldest pieces of alliterative poetry (since the Conquest) in existence. This is easily seen by its resemblance in language to " William of Palerne," and I should place it *earlier* than " Piers the Plowman." It can hardly be *later,* as it is found in the same MS. with the *earliest* copy of the *earliest* version of that poem. We may safely date it not later than A.D. 1360, but I prefer rather to date it about 1350, for its metre is of a more rugged and earlier character than even that of "William of Palerne." And I may here pause to remark that the law of progress in alliterative poetry is from lines cast in a loose mould to lines cast in a strict one; from lines with *two* alliterated letters to lines with *three,* and in very late instances, to lines with *four ;* [1] from lines with irregular feet to those in which extreme regularity makes the iteration of like initial sounds somewhat forced and monotonous. Of course some writers were more careless than others, but these principles may safely guide us to some extent, and the fact that *two* letters so frequently suffice to the alliteration in our fragment is decidedly a mark of antiquity. See, e.g. lines 2—11 ; the *sixth* line alone has *three* words beginning with the same letter. In l. 9, the *v* answers to *f ;* [2] in l. 12, we have the unusual number of *four* rime-letters.

§ 6. Before proceeding to the subject-matter, it will be convenient to consider the dialect in which the poem is written. The remark in my " Essay," that the best examples of alliterative metre

[1] P. Plowman, A-text; pref. p. xxii. Some of the latest examples of alliterative verse relapse into irregularity, owing to lack of skill on the part of the authors.

[2] This peculiarity I have nowhere else observed, except in Piers the Plowman and the Deposition of Richard II. In l. 448 of our poem we have *verreili* answering to *figure ;* but the (Southern) scribe has changed *figure* into *rigore.*

are to be found in the *northern* and *western* dialects, holds true in the present instance, the southern forms in the poem being due to a southern scribe. But I would here wish to remind the reader that examples of mixed dialect require great caution. It is usual to assume that the admixture of dialectal forms is due to the scribe. But such is by no means necessarily the case. There are *three* solutions that will account for such a result, and not *one alone*. The three solutions are these. Either (1) the author may have tried to write in a dialect not his own ; or (2) he may have both spoken and written a mixed dialect; or (3) the author may have composed in one dialect, whilst the scribe afterwards altered many of the author's forms to those of another dialect with which he was himself more familiar. Of course the third of these solutions is generally the true one, but it must not be universally adopted ; for examples of the other theories, though rare, are still actually to be found. The *first* theory is true for "Lancelot of the Laik" and for some poems by Scottish authors, who (such was the deference paid to Chaucer's language) actually affected Anglicisms, as has been pointed out by Mr J. A. H. Murray. The *second* theory is true for "Piers the Plowman," of which at least thirty MSS. are written in a *mixed* dialect,[1] which must have originated with the author. But, in the present case, the *third* or usual theory is obviously the right one ; for the southernizing tendencies of the scribe are well-known, from the numerous other pieces which he has written out; whilst the more northern forms found must be original, owing to the known fact of alliterative poems being generally in a northern or western dialect. The poem was, I believe, originally in a West-Midland dialect, but its forms have been frequently altered by the Southern scribe. It is, therefore, all the more interesting to notice the non-southern forms which he has left intact. I proceed to give a general account of the forms found.

The plurals of the substantives end in -*es*, as *lippes*, 49 ;[2] but one

---

[1] P. Plowman, B-text; pref. p. xliii. In pref. to A-text, p. xvi, I have inadvertently assumed the Vernon MS. to be the best *in every respect ;* I should have said, in every respect but the dialect, which the scribe has improved and made *more uniformly Southern.*

[2] The numbers refer to the lines.

plural ends in *-us*, viz. *gultus*, 249 ; and one in *-en*, viz. *honden*, 272. Other plurals worth notice are *winter*, 3 ; *niȝt*, 6 ; *foote*, 14 ; *childre*, 493 ; *schon*, 423. There is one genitive plural in *-ene*, viz. *schalkene*, 510.

In the comparatives of adjectives and adverbs, the ending *-ore* (*-or*) is found, as : *dimmore*, 183 ; *lengore*, 137 ; *freschore*, 595 ; *feirore*, 649 ; *heuior*, 592. The same is found in the A-text of Piers Plowman, by the same scribe ; cf. *febelore*, P. Pl. A. i. 160 ; *hardore*, i. 165. Observe also the form *ȝernloker*, 593.

As regards pronouns, we find *heo* or *he* for *she*, 83, 87 ; for *he*, 97 ; and for *they*, 283 ; the gen. pl. is *heore*, 18, or *here*, 30 ; the dat. pl. is *heom*, 130 ; the acc. pl. *hem*, 31. But we find also the nom. *þei*, 244. The acc. of *ȝe* (ye) is *ou* or *ow ;* we find also *hise*, pl. 24 ; *þis*, pl. 29 ; *þo*, pl. 60 ; *vr* or *vre* (our), and *or* or *oure* (your) ; cf. P. Plowm. A. The word *selue*, pl. means *very*, 303.

The infinitive mood of verbs ends in *-en*, as *rikenen*, 76, but more commonly in *-e*, as *here*, 74, *fare*, 63 ; both forms are found close together, as *lenden and lihte*, 81. I have observed no infinitives in *-ie* or *-y* (Southern forms), but the Northern form *ha* (for *have*) occurs twice, 351, 578. In the present tense, the 2nd pers. sing. ends in *-est*, as *berest*, 40 ; but we find also *þou ȝemes*, 310, *þou wendes*, 420. The 3rd pers. sing. ends in *-es*, as *askes*, 7, *biddes*, 22, *spekes*, 38 ; but we find also *greteþ*, 347, *bereþ*, 396 ; cf. *me þinkeþ*, 6, with *me forþinkes*, 487. The plural ends in *-en* or *-e*, as *folewen*, 8, *carpen*, 175, *carke*, 30 ; but we actually find *-es* in *bydes*, 468. I have my doubts about *ȝe clepeþ* (379) being the genuine reading, though *beþ* occurs in l. 409. In the past tense, 2nd person, we find *-est* in *souȝtest*, *eodest*, 4, *lengedest*, 429 ; but observe *þou souȝtes*, 431, *þou slouȝ*, 433, *þou come*, 434, *þou toke*, 438 ; and note how *þou wast* (425) is changed to *þou weore*, 428. In l. 223 we find *þou for-ȝaf*. The following are examples of the past tense singular, most of which may be found in the glossary ; STRONG VERBS,[1] DI- VISION I, CLASS I, *bar, bad, breek, ȝaf, heold, lay, speek, com ;* CLASS III, *stod* (359), *tok ;* DIV. II, CLASS I, *to-barst, fond, halp, starf ;* CLASS II, *ros* (268) ; CLASS III, *bed, fleyȝ, lees, say* (*sayȝ, seȝe, sauh, seiȝ,*

[1] See Specimens of Early English, ed. Morris.

seih), *tei* (*teiȝ*) ;—WEAK VERBS, *hopede*, 59, *lente*, *sende*, *lafte*, *hedde*, *þouȝte*. The plural generally ends in *-en* or *-e*, as *ladden*, *lengede*, 16 ; but we sometimes find the final *-e* dropped, as in *bosked*, *vn-housed* (before *hem*, 13, 455). Now if we compare the present poem with the schemes of conjugation of regular and irregular West-Midland verbs in Mr Morris's preface to his edition of Early English Alliterative Poems, we can find examples of nearly all the endings which he gives, as thus. Regular Verbs, pres. sing. *þonke*, *wendes*, *askes* ; pl. *carpen*, *mene*[*n*], *melen* ; past sing. *wepte*, *souȝtes*, *fulwede* ; pl. *passeden*. Irregular Verbs, pres. sing. *hete*, —, *fonges* ; pl. *slen* ; past tense, —, (*þou*) *for-ȝaf*, *bad* ; pl. *flowen*. Even still more significant are the endings in *-es* in the plural of the imperative mood, which in a Southern dialect would become *-eþ* ; yet the scribe gives us *gos*, *proues*, 373, *holdes*, 492, *þenkes*, 493. The present participles have the Southern endings *-inge* or *-inde*, as *honginge*, 205, *cominge*, 206, *romynge*, 275, *stremynge*, 560, *comynge*, 562, *lenginde*, 20, *houwynde*, 294, *folewynde*, 551. There are also examples of nouns substantive in *-ing*, as *crucifiing*, 241, *lustnynge*, 164, *comynge*, 421, *schindringe*, 513. The past participles of strong verbs end in *-en*, as *hoten*, *holden*, *stiken*, *bounden*, *taken*, *nomen*. In P. Plowman (A) we often find *d* altered to *t* in the past participles of weak verbs, and the scribe has frequently made the same alteration here ; as in *werret*, *scaþet*, *I-bosket*, *a-bascht*, *haspet*, *Iugget* (251), *braset*, *a-semblet*, *wondet*, *wemmet*. We even find the same in the past tense, as in *fondet*, 12. This peculiarity occurs even in nouns, as *fert*, *þousent*, *bert*, *wynt*, for *ferd*, *þousend*, *berd*, *wynd*. Past participles are generally found without the prefix *I-*, but we have also *I-ben*, *I-blesset*, &c. ; a list of these being given in the Glossary. We find *Ichul*, *icholde*, for *ich wol*, *ich wolde*; and the second personal pronoun joined on to the verb, as in *hastou*, *hettestou*, *trouwestou*, *woldestou*. Verbs occur with the negative prefix, as *nis*, *nare*, *nas*, *nul*, *nedden*, *nuste*, for *ne is*, *ne are*, *ne was*, *ne wol*, *ne hedden*, *ne wuste*. The free use of negatives is well exemplified by the l. 342—

þis oþer two nare none · in no maner þinge.

Verbs occur with the prefix *to-*, as *to-barst*, *to-borsten*, *to-clouen*, *to-hurles ;* only in the last case (*al to-hurles*) is the adverb *al* superadded. Other noteworthy points are the occurrence of *wepte* (not *wep*) as the past tense of *wepen*, 647 ; whilst besides *fel*, as the past tense of *fallen*, we find the curious form *felde*, shewing that the correct reading of the puzzling line in Havelok (2698) is probably— þat he [ne] felden so dos þe gres—i. e. that they did not *fall* as does the grass. We may also note the use of *was* for *who was*, 19 ; *enes*, *atenes ;* the verb *worþe*, 146 ; *forte* for *forto* (as in P. Pl. A.) ; *boto*, 300, beside the full form *boþe two*, 697 ; the phrase þreo *mauer enkes*, 194 ; *no-skunus* for *nos kunes ; eornen* for *rennen*, 275, &c. The numerous forms from the verb *ben* (to be) are given in the Glossary ; thus we find in the pl. indic. present *ben, beon, beþ, beoþ*, and *aren. Bi* is written for *be*, as in William of Palerne; but a still more remarkable form is *he beos*, 216, which is quite a Northern form. So also is *out-wiþ* for *wiþ-out.* Some of the words in the Glossary most worthy of remark are *allynge, blencheden, boskes, bounen, carke, demayen, derue, faus, felde, feye, flote, folfulsened, for-set, geyn, greiþli, gretnede, inne* (vb.), *keueren, limpe, luttulde, mallen, note, of-fouȝten, of-scutered, out-wiþ, pallede, res, roungede, schalkene, schindringe, seyne, slauht, sound, sporn, sputison, teis, teiȝ, þroly, vmbe, vnsauht, wasscheles, wawes, whappede, whucche, wustest*, and several others. It is a piece well worth attention from a philological point of view, as well as for its curiosity.

§ 7. The five principal Arthurian Romances are set down in the following order by Sir F. Madden, in his " Syr Gawayne," Pref. p. x.[1]

1. "The History of the Holy Graal," which tells of Joseph of Arimathea, and how he brought the holy vessel [2] to England.

2. " Merlin."

3. " Lancelot of the Lake."

4. "The Quest of the Holy Graal."

5. " Le Mort Artus," or " Morte Darthur."

[1] See Mr Furnivall's Introduction to "Merline," in Bishop Percy's Folio MS., ed. Hales and Furnivall, vol. i. p. 411.

[2] "This, said he [Christ] is the holy dish wherein I ate the lamb on Sher- thursday ;" Malory's Morte Darthur ed. Sir E. Strachey, bk. xvii. ch. 20.

Our poem contains only the earlier portion of the *first* of these, and its contents may be thus epitomized. The portion within square brackets is lost.

[After our Lord's entombment, Joseph of Arimathea was seized by the Jews, and imprisoned in a dungeon without a window, where he remained for forty-two years, till released by Vespasian.] After his release, he tells Vespasian that the time of his imprisonment has seemed but three days. Being first baptized himself, he proceeds to baptize Vespasian and fifty others; after which Vespasian wreaks vengeance on the Jews who had imprisoned Joseph. In obedience to a divine voice, Joseph, with his wife, his son Josephes (or Josaphe) and a company of fifty people, leaves Jerusalem, and arrives at Sarras, taking with him the Holy Graal, or Sacred Dish containing Christ's blood, which is carried inside an ark or box. Joseph tries to convert Evalak, the king of Sarras, at the same time declaring the doctrine of the Trinity. The king provides for the wants of Joseph's company, but has his doubts about the truth of the doctrine. The following night, he is converted by two visions. In the first he sees three stems growing from one trunk, and appearing to coalesce into one; an emblem of the Trinity in Unity.[1] In the second he sees a child pass through a solid wall without any injury to the wall, an emblem of Christ's spotless Incarnation. Josaphe, the son of Joseph, also sees a vision; for, on peering into the Grail-Ark, he beholds Christ upon the cross, and five angels with the instruments of the Passion; afterwards appear eleven more angels, whilst Christ seems to descend from the cross, and to stand beside an altar, upon the one end of which are the Lance and Three Nails, and upon the other the DISH WITH THE BLOOD (the HOLY GRAIL). Christ then ordains Josaphe bishop, and bids him go to Evalak's palace. A clerk is appointed by King Evalak to dispute with Joseph, but is miraculously struck dumb, whilst at the same time his eyes fly out of his head. Evalak repairs to a temple of idols, hoping to secure the clerk's recovery, but the idols are

---

[1] "After a while the three trees touched one another, then began to incorporate and confound their several natures in a single trunk."—*Legend of the Cross*, in Curious Myths of the Middle Ages, by S. Baring-Gould; ii. 117.

xvi   PREFACE.

powerless. Soon after, a messenger arrives to tell Evalak that his
land has been invaded by Tholomer, king of Babylon, whereupon
Evalak prepares for war. Before he sets out, Joseph and Josaphe
have a private interview with Evalak, wherein Joseph tells the king
that he is acquainted with all his previous history, after which
Josaphe gives Evalak a shield with a red cross upon it, telling him to
pray to Christ in the hour of peril. In the first encounter, Tholomer's men are successful, but lose their tents. Evalak then
collects more men, and is joined by his wife's brother, Seraphe, with
five hundred men. In the next battle, king Evalak and duke
Seraphe perform wonders, but at last Seraphe is wounded sorely,
and Evalak made prisoner. As Evalak is being led to death, he remembers Josaphe's advice; he uncovers the shield with the red
cross, and prays to Christ. An angel comes to the rescue, in the
outward form of a White Knight, who slays Tholomer, heals
Seraphe, mounts Evalak upon Tholomer's horse, and helps him to
achieve a complete victory; after which he vanishes away. Meanwhile Joseph has an interview with Evalak's queen, who was at
heart a Christian, and whose early history is related. Evalak
returns home, and is baptized, being named Mordreins; Seraphe is
also baptized, with the name of Naciens. Joseph further baptizes
five thousand of Evalak's subjects, and abides at Sarras, whilst
Josaphe and Naciens set out upon a missionary journey, the Holy
Grail being left at Sarras, in the charge of two of Joseph's company. The poem here ceases, with a brief reference to the subse-
quent imprisonment of Josaphe by the king of North Wales, and
his release by Mordreins (Evalak).

The real subject of the story is therefore the adventures of
Joseph of Arimathea at the court of Evalak, king of Sarras, with
the episode of king Evalak's shield. The object of the poet clearly
was to translate so much of the legend of "Joseph" as most pleased
his fancy, and we may allow that he has fairly acquitted himself in
the task. Though following in the main a French original, he seems
to have had a fair command of language; many of his lines are
terse and striking, and he seems to be particularly at home in describ-
ing battle scenes; see e. g. ll. 498—517, 531—534, 584—600. Such
lines as

Schon schene vppon schaft · schalkene blod (510),

Al to-hurles þe helm · and þe hed vnder (533),

and

Wiþ þe deþ in his hals · dounward he duppes (534),

are really good ; and there is a very sufficient vigour in the expression

maden þer a siker werk · and slowen hem vp clene [1] (605).

§ 8. The story of Evalak's shield is related to Galahad by " the white knight " in the Romance of the Quest of the Saint Graal, from whence it was inserted by Malory in his " Morte Darthur," book xiii, ch. 10. I here give the original version of it from " La Queste del Saint Graal" (supposed to have been written by Walter Map) as edited by Mr Furnivall for the Roxburghe Club in 1864 ; pp. 27—30.

"Galaad," fait li chiualers, "il auint apres la passion notre singnour .xlii. ans, que ioseph d'abarimathie, li gentiex chiualers qui despendi notre seignour de la crois, se parti de la chite de iherusalem entrui grant partie de ses parens. Et tant errerent par le commandement de notre signour qu'il vinrent en la chite de sarras que li rois Eualac, qui lors yert sarrasins, tenoit a chel tans que Ioseph y uint. Auint que li rois eualac gerroia .j. sien voisin, riche homme. Tholomes ot non. quant eualac se fu apprestes sour tholomes, que sa terre li demandoit, Josaphes li fiex ioseph lui dist. 'que s'il aloit en bataille si desconseillies comme il estoit, qu'il seroit desconfis.· Et honnis par son anemi.' 'Et que m'en loes vous,' dist Eualac. 'che vous dirai iou bien' fait il, lors li commencha a traire auant les poins de la nouuele loy, et la veritei des Euuangeles. et del crucefiement notre signour. et del resussitement de ihesu crist lui dist la veritei. et lui fist un escu ou quel il fist vne crois de chendal, et li dist, 'rois Eualac, ore te mousterrai appartement comment tu porras connoistre la forche et la virtu du urai crucefi. Et il est voirs [2] que tholomes ara sour toi soignourie iij. jours et iij. nuis. Et tant te fera que me te mettra juskes a paour de mort. Mais quant tu verras que tu ne porras escaper, lors descouuerras la

(marginal notes:) 42 years after Christ's death, Joseph of Arimathien and his relatives went by God's command to Sarras, the city of King Evalach, who was warring against Tholome, and Josephes tells Evalach that if he fights as he is, he will be beaten by his enemy; to prevent which, Josephes expounds the Christian faith to him, and makes him a shield with a cross of red cendal on it, which, when in fear of death, he is to uncover, and to pray to Christ.

---

[1] It is to be regretted that so many of our early poets are nameless. All that can be done is to investigate if any two poems are by the same author. The author of "William of Palerne" could have written lines like these, but there is too much dissimilarity in the metre to admit of the identification.

[2] MS. vous.

This Evalach
does when in
danger of death
in battle; sees a
bleeding crucified
man on the
Shield, and gains
the victory
thereby.
On his return
to Sarras,
Evalach tells his
people of
Josephes' truth,
and Nasciens is
baptized.

The Shield and
Cross also restore
a man his lost
hand,

and the Cross
disappears and
re-appears on the
Shield.

Evalach is then
baptized,

and Josephes and
his father come to
Great Britain and
are imprisoned.

On which
Mordreins (or
Evalach) and
Nasciens invade
Britain, and free
Joseph,

and remain
and serve him.

On his deathbed
Evalach asks
him

crois. et diras, biaus sires diex, de la qui moit je
poch le signe, Jetes moi sain et sauf de chest camp. a
recheuoir uotre foy et votre creanche.' a tant s'en
parti li roys Eualac, et ala a host sour tholomes. Et il
li auint tout ensi comme chil li dist. Quant il se vit
en tel peril qu'il quidoit vraiement mourir, il descouuri
son escu. Et vit en milieu vn homme crucefie qui tous
estoit sanglens, si dist les paroles que josaphas li auoit
enseignies, dont il ot victorie et houneur. Et fu jetes
des mains a sen anemi. Et vint au dessus de tholomes.
Et de tous ses hounmes. Et quant il fu reuenus a sa
chitei a sarras : si dist au peuple la veritei qu'il auoit
trouuee en josephee. Et manifesta tant l'entree des
crestiens, que nasciens rechut batesme. Et en che
qu'il se crestienoit, auint ke vns hons passoit par deuant
aus qui auoit le poing caupe. et portoit son poing en
s'autre main, et josephes l'apela od soy et chil y uint.
Et si tost comme il ot atouchiet a la crois qui en l'escu
estoit. Si se trouua ichil tous garis del poing qu'il
auoit perdu, et encore en auint il vne autre auenture
mult merueilleuse : que li crois que en l'escu estoit, se
parti, et s'ahiert au brach d'enemie en tel maniere que
ains puis ne fu veue en l'escu. Lors rechut eualac
baptesme. et deuint serians Jesu crist. et ot puis notres
sires en grant amour et en grant reuerence. et fist
garder l'escu mout signourieument. apres auint quant
iosephes se fu partis de sarras, entre lui et son pere.
et il furent venu en la grant bertaigne. si trouuerent .j.
roy. Cruel et felon. qui andeus les enprisouna, et od
lui grant partie de crestiens. quant josephes fu enprisounes. Tost en ala lonch la nouuele. Car allours
n'auoit homme el monde de greignour renoumee. Et
tantost comme li rois mordains en oy parler. si semonst
ses hommes et ses gens, entre lui et nascien son serouge.
Et s'en uinrent. En la grant bertaigne sour chelui roy
qui iosephe tenoit en prison, et les destrainsent et con-
fundirent tous chiaus du pais, si que en la terre fu
espandue sainte crestientes. Et il amerent tant iosephe
qu'il ne s'en vaurrent partir del pais. ains remensent
auoec lui. Et li seruoient en tous les lieus ou il aloit.
Et quant che fu coze que iosephes fu au lit mortel.
Eualac counut qu'il li couuenoit partir de chest sieucle.
et vint deuant lui, si ploura mult tenrement. Et dist,
' sire, puis ke vous me laissies, ore remainrai Je ausi
comme tous seus en chest pais, ke pour l'amor de uous
auoie ma terre laissie et ma nascion, pour dieu, puis k'il
vous couuient partir de chest siecle, laissies moi de vous

aucune ensaigne qui apres vous me fache ramenbranche.'
'Sire,' fist iosephes, 'je le vous ferai.' lors com- for some
remembrance
of him.
mencha a penser quel cose il li porroit ballier. et
quant il ot grant piecche pense. si dist. 'rois Mordains, Joseph tells him
fai moi aporter ichel escu que jou te ballai quant tu to bring the
Shield, and, when
alas en la bataille sour tholomes.' Et li rois le fist, ensi it is brought,
Joseph bleeds at
comme chil qui le faisoit porter od soi en tous les lieus the nose,
ou il aloit, si fist aporter l'escu : a chel point qu'il fu
aportes, auint k'il saina mult durement parmi le nes, si
que iosephes ne pooit estankier. et il prist maintenant and makes a
cross with his
l'escu, et j fist de chelui meisme sanc vne crois, si com blood on the
vous le vees. Et bien sachies que ch'est chil escus Shield,
and tells
meismes dont ie vous cont que vous portes. Et quant Mordreins he
will leave him
il ot faite la crois telle comme vous poes veoir. il li the Shield in
remembrance of
dist, 'ves chi chest escu ke je vous laisse en ramem- him,
branche de moy. Car vous saues bien que ceste crois
est faite de mon sanc. Si sera tous iours ausi freche et
ausi uermelle comme vous le poes ore-endroit veoir.
tant comme li escus durra. ne il ne saura mie tost pour
chou que nus iamais a son col ne le pendera pour qu'il but no one is to
hang it on his
soit chiualers qu'il ne s'en repenche. Juskes a tant que neck till Galahad
comes.
galaad li boins chiualers, li derrains del linaige nacien,
le pendera au sien col. Et pour chou ne soit nus si
hardis qui a son col le pende, se chil non a qui dieus l'a
destineie. Si ra telle occoison, que tout ausi comme en
l'escu ont este veuwes meruellies grandes plus que
autres, tout ausi verra on en lui meruelleuses proueches.
Et plus haute uie que en autre chiualer.' 'I'vis qu'il Mordreins asks
where he shall
est ensi,' fait li rois, 'ke si boine ramenbranche me leave the Shield,
laires, dont me dites, si'l vous plaist, ou jou lairai chest
escu. Car jou nauroie mout qu'il fuist mis eu tel lieu
ou li boins chiualers le trouuaist.' 'Dont vous dirai and Joseph says,
in the place
je,' fait iosephes, 'que vous feres la ou nasciens se prin where Nasciens
is buried,
mettre apres sa mort, si metes l'escu, car illoec uenra li
boins chiualers au chieunquisme iour qu'il aura rechut for Galahad shall
come on the fifth
l'ordene de cheualerie.' si est tout ensi auenu com il day after he is
knighted.
dit. Car al quint iour que uous fustes chiualers,
venistes vous en ceste abeie ou naciens gist. si vous ai
ore tout contei, pour queles auentures sont auenues as
chiualers plains de fol quidier qui sour cestui defense,
et voloient porter l'escu qui a lui ni ert otroies, fors que
a vous." quant il ot tout chou contei, si s'esuanui en tel The White
Knight vanishes
maniere qu'il ne sot qu'il hiert deuenus. ne de quel when he has told
this history.
part il ert tourneis.

§ 9. ACCOUNT OF THE PROSE "LYFE OF JOSEPH."

The "Lyfe of Joseph of Armathy," printed by Wynkyn de
Worde,[1] corresponds tolerably closely to the account of his Life as
given in Capgrave's "Nova Legenda Angliæ," who perhaps borrowed it from John of Glastonbury; see Hearne's "Johannis
Glastoniensis Chronica." Capgrave's work is known to be princi-
pally taken from John of Tynemouth, but I have not been able to
ascertain whether he took from him the legend of Joseph in particular. If it be not found in John of Tynemouth, then the
probability of Capgrave having here followed John of Glastonbury
becomes almost a certainty. The first part of the story, down to p.
30, l. 23, follows the Apocryphal Gospel of Nicodemus; of the
rest, the original Latin is quoted at length from Capgrave, and
collated with Hearne's edition of John of Glastonbury, in the Note
on p. 68. This account by John of Glastonbury seems to have
been made up from several sources, and the whole matter is well
treated in Archbishop Ussher's "Britannicarum Ecclesiarum An-
tiquitates," printed at Dublin in 1639. This work enables us to
trace some of these sources, more or less exactly. Thus, in the latter part of the account, printed on pp. 68—70, the portion from
"Post hec" to "gallias venit" (p. 69, l. 1) is quoted by Ussher (p.
16) as extant in a great table (ingens tabula) of Glastonbury antiquities in the possession of William, son of Thomas Howard,
duke of Norfolk. The next piece, from "Dispersis enim" down to
"prefecit" (p. 69, l. 7) is from William of Malmesbury; see Gul.
Malmesb. de Antiq. Glaston. Ecclesiæ, p. 5, included in Hearne's
edition of Adam de Domerham; Oxon. 1727. The next piece, from
"Venerunt" to "rege aruirago" (p. 69, l. 35) professes to be from
the book which is called the Holy Graal ("Sanctum Graal"); cf.
Ussher, p. 17, where the "Sanctum Graal" is also referred to.
The next piece, from "anno ab incarnacione" down to "fidelium"
(p. 70, l. 22), is again from William of Malmesbury, with the
exception of the four verses, which Ussher calls "barbari illi ver-

---

[1] See the description in Herbert's Ames, vol. i. p. 232.

siculi, ex Chronicis quibusdam de rege Arvirago agentibus citati" (Brit. Eccl. Ant. p. 16). A portion of this passage is also quoted, from the Glastonbury records, by John of Tynemouth (Ussher, p. 18). The succeeding paragraph is founded upon the Arthur romances, as John of Glastonbury himself tells us. He cites the passage "where a certain hermit expounds to Walwain the mystery of a certain fountain;" and a second passage from near the beginning of the Quest (*inquisitio*) of the Seint Graal, where "a white knight relates to Galahad the mystery of a certain wonderful shield." The former of these references I cannot verify; but it probably is to be found in one of the later Romances, perhaps in Lancelot. The latter is the identical passage from the "Queste" printed above, p. xvii.

After this, we have an extract from Melkin,[1] of whom nothing seems to be known except that he lived before Merlin, although Spelman is bold enough to say that he flourished about A.D. 550; see Spelman's "Concilia, &c. in re ecclesiarum orbis Britannici," vol. i. p. 6. This passage is also found in MSS. Cotton, Titus D. vii, fol. 29 *b*, and Arundel 220, fol. 274; but the MSS. have in addition the paragraph "Ex quo apostoli," &c., printed on p. 71, which nearly agrees with the account in John of Tynemouth; see Ussher, pp. 18 and 974.

The point where this "Lyfe of Joseph" ceases to follow John of Glastonbury is marked by note 12 on p. 69. The remaining eight lines briefly refer to the story of Celydomus or Celydoine as told in the Romance of the Seynt Graal; see the notes on p. 67.

§ 10. ACCOUNT OF THE PIECE " DE SANCTO JOSEPH."

This, the third piece in the volume, is from "The Kalendre of the New Legende of Englande," printed by Pynson in 1516, and described in Herbert's Ames, vol. i. p. 261. It is a mere epitome of Capgrave's account; see the notes on p. 72.

---

[1] Printed also in Johannis Glastoniensis Chronica, ed. Hearne, p. 30. Melkin is possibly the same as "Mewynus, the Bryton chronicler," mentioned in Hardyng's Chronicle, ch. 1., and in ch. xliii, where MSS. have the various readings *Newinus, Nenius,* and *Neninus:* which look very like Nennius.

§ 11. ACCOUNT OF THE VERSE "LYFE OF JOSEPH."

This piece was printed by Pynson in 1520, and is a rather singular one. It was composed either in the year 1502 or soon after,[1] by some one very familiar with Glastonbury, and with the most evident object of encouraging all men to make offerings at the shrine of St Joseph; we may therefore feel tolerably sure that the author was a monk of Glastonbury. A short account of it is given in Hazlitt's Handbook of Early English Literature, p. 312.

The title-page (p. 35) bears the arms of Glastonbury, thus described by Ussher (Britan. Eccles. Antiq. p. 29), who quotes from the account given by William Good, a Jesuit born at Glastonbury in the reign of Henry VIII. "Antiqua arma Glastoniensis Monasterii . . . sunt hujusmodi. Scutum album, in quo per longum erigitur stipes crucis viridis & nudosæ, & de latere ad latus extenduntur brachia seu rami crucis stipiti consimilia. Sparguntur guttæ sanguinis per omnem arcam scuti. Utrinque ad latera stipitis, & sub alis crucis, ponitur ampulla inaurata. Et hæc semper denominabantur insignia Sancti Josephi, qui ibi habitâsse piè credebatur, & fortassè sepultus esse." The knotted cross evidently refers to the legend of St Joseph's thorny staff, the drops of blood denote his receiving the blood of Christ in the Holy Grail, and the two cruets (as they are called in l. 32 of the poem) are the "duo fassula" mentioned in the book of Melkin (see p. 70, l. 3 from the bottom), which resulted from the duplication of the Grail of the original legend.

The poem is written in eight-line stanzas, and the metre is as poor as in most of the poems of the reign of Henry VII. In the first 216 lines, we have an account similar to that in Capgrave, the "Graal" portion of the story commencing at l. 113 and ending at l. 192. The latter part of the poem is a special appeal to the faithful to visit St Joseph's shrine, and recites the numerous miracles which had just taken place, chiefly in the month of April, 1502. Several places in the neighbourhood of Glastonbury are mentioned, viz. Dolting, Wells, Banwell, Ilchester, Yeovil, Milborne Port,

[1] See the notes to ll. 234 and 289.

Comton, and Pilton. Of these, "Dulting" and "Piltune" are mentioned in the Charter of King Ini which contains grants to Glastonbury Abbey.[1] The author proves Glastonbury to be the " holyest erth of england " (l. 369), by appealing to a story in the life of St David; cf. note on p. 73. This story is told by William of Malmesbury ; see Hardy's edition, vol. i. p. 38, Gale's edition, vol. i. p. 299, or p. 30 of the Rev. J. Sharpe's translation ; or it may be read in John of Glastonbury, ed. Hearne, p. 2. It is also repeated in an inscription upon a metal plate formerly affixed to a column which was erected to mark the exact size of the chapel at Glastonbury before St David added the chancel to it. A *facsimile* of this inscription is given at p. 9 of Spelman's " Concilia," &c. tom. i. ; it is also printed in Hearne's History and Antiquities of Glaston- bury, p. 118 ; see also p. 20. Lastly, the author alludes to the marvellous walnut-tree, growing "hard by the place where kynge Arthur was founde," and the three hawthorn-trees at Werrall or Weary-all-hill ; although the story is generally told of *one* such tree only. *the* Glastonbury thorn,[2] which grew up on the spot where St Joseph stuck his staff of hawthorn-wood into the ground after his arrival. He then concludes with " A Praysyng to Joseph," and an Officium.[3]

§ 12. GLASTONBURY ABBEY, AND THE INTRODUCTION OF CHRISTIANITY INTO BRITAIN.

This is not the place to enter into a subject so full of interest as the history of Glastonbury Abbey ; but I may at least observe that the very first page of Dugdale's Monasticon Anglicanum contains an account which assumes the truth of the legend of the arrival in Britain of Joseph of Arimathea, as well as of several other statements in John of Glastonbury. It is therefore worth while to quote it in connection with the present subject.

[1] Printed in Willelmi Malmesbiriensis Gesta Regum Anglorum, ed. T. D. Hardy, vol. i. p. 51.

[2] See an engraving of it in Knight's Old England, vol. i. p. 133, and a notice of the legend at p. 131. See also Chambers' Book of Days, vol. ii. p. 758: Hearne's History and Antiquities of Glastonbury; Collinson's History of Somersetshire, vol. ii. p. 265 ; Brand's Antiquities, ed. W. C. Hazlitt, vol. iii. 358, &c.

[3] There is an Officium somewhat like this printed in Hearne's edition of John of Glastonbury, p. 4 ; see also the Acta Sanctorum, xvii Martii.

Dugdale's account commences as follows :

"About sixty-three years after the Incarnation of our Lord, St Joseph of Arimathea, accompanied by eleven other disciples of St Philip, was despatched by that Apostle into Britain, to introduce in the place of barbarous and bloody rites, long exercised by the bigotted and besotted druids, the meek and gentle system of Christianity. They succeeded in obtaining from Arviragus, the British king, permission to settle in a small island, then rude and uncultivated, and to each of the twelve was assigned for his subsistence, a certain portion of land called a hide, comprising a district, denominated to this day THE TWELVE HIDES OF GLASTON. Their boundaries, as well as the names of the principal places contained in them, will be found in the Appendix [1] (nos. i. and ii.). They enjoyed all the immunities of regal dignity, from ancient times and the first establishment of christianity in this land. One peculiar privilege which this church possessed by the grant of king Canute (App. num. lxvi.), was that no subject could enter this district without the permission of the abbot and convent. It now includes the following parishes ; Glastonbury St Benedict, Glastonbury St John, Baltonsbury, Bradley, Mere, West-Pennard, and North-Wotton.

"The name by which the island was distinguished by the Britons was *Ynswytryn*, or the Glassy Island, from the colour of the stream which surrounded it. Afterwards it obtained the name of Avallon, either from Aval, an apple, in which fruit it abounded ; or from Avallon, a British chief, to whom it formerly belonged. The Saxons finally called it Glæsting-byrig.

"Here St Joseph, who is considered by the monkish historians as the first abbot, erected, to the honour of the Virgin Mary, of wreathed twigs, the first Christian oratory in England."

In this account, the word *Ynswytryn* should rather be spelt *Ynyswytryn*, the former element being the Welsh *ynys*, or Gaelic *innis* (sometimes corrupted into *inch*), an island, whilst the latter is connected with the Welsh *gwydr*, Latin *vitrum*. The Welsh word for apple is *afal*, whilst *afallwyn*, an orchard, comes still closer to Avalon ; but the derivation is, perhaps, doubtful. The word is spelt *Aualun* in Laʒamon, vol. iii. p. 144.[2] The Saxon name should

---

[1] I. e. the Appendix to the Monasticon.

[2] " This fair Avalon—

> 'Where falls not hail, or rain, or any snow,
> Nor ever wind blows loudly ; but it lies
> Deep-meadow'd, happy, fair with orchard-lawns
> And bowery hollows crown'd with summer sea,'

is the Isle of the Blessed of the Kelts. Tzetze and Procopius attempt to

be spelt Glæstinga-burig, where Glæstinga is a genitive plural, so that the word means "the borough of the sons of Glæst;" this disposes of the supposition that glæs (glass) corresponds to the Welsh element -wytryn, yet the coincidence is certainly curious. The chief point to be noticed about Glastonbury Abbey is its proved antiquity, even if the story of the coming of Joseph be set aside. "Canterbury and York have no connection with the early British Church; but go to Glastonbury, and there what people simply dream of in other places becomes a real and living fact. Somersetshire between Axe and Parret was conquered by the Christian Cenwealh; Somersetshire beyond Parret was conquered by the famous lawgiver Ine. Unlike their forefathers in their heathen days, but exactly like the Christian Teutons in their continental conquests, the West-Saxon conquerors now spared, honoured, and enriched the great ecclesiastical establishment of the conquered. The ancient church of wood or wicker, which legend spoke of as the first temple reared on British soil to the honour of Christ, was preserved as a hallowed relic, even after a greater church of stone was built by Dunstan to the east of it. And though not a fragment of either of those buildings still remains, yet each alike is represented in the peculiar arrangements of that mighty and now fallen minster. The wooden church of the Briton is represented by the famous Lady Chapel, better known as the chapel of Saint Joseph; the stone church of the West-Saxon is represented by the vast Abbey church itself. Nowhere else can we see the works of the conquerors and the works of the conquered thus standing, though but in a figure, side by side. Nowhere else, among all the churches of England, can we find one which can thus trace up its uninterrupted being to the days before the Teuton had set foot upon British soil. The legendary burial-place of Arthur, the real burying-place of Eadgar and the two Eadmunds, stands

localize it, and suppose that the Land of Souls is Britain; but in this they are mistaken; as also are those who think to find Avalon at Glastonbury. Avalon is the Isle of Apples—a name reminding one of the Garden of the Hesperides in the far western seas, with its tree of golden apples in the midst."—*The Fortunate Isles;* in Curious Myths of the Middle Ages, by S. Baring-Gould, vol. ii. p. 270.

alone among English minsters as the one link which really does bind us to the ancient Church of the Briton and the Roman." [1]

In like manner, the real significance of the legend of St Joseph seems to me to be this, that the first missionaries of Christianity actually arrived in Britain at an early period, although (as will appear presently) this supposition rests upon mere guess, and is unsupported by any evidence. The question of the first introduction of Christianity into Britain has been frequently discussed, and Gildas, in particular, has been appealed to as saying that it was introduced in the time of Tiberius, whereas he says nothing of the kind. Various attempts have been made to establish a probability that Christian missionaries had really arrived here before the time of the supposed conversion of king Lucius (Beda, Eccl. Hist. Bk. i. ch. 4), the date of which has been settled by twenty-six writers in as many ways. [2] Mr Beale Poste, for instance, in his Britannic - Researches, pp. 385—410, contends that the mission of Aristobulus is undoubtedly the best authenticated as the first which took place, this Aristobulus being the same as is mentioned by St Paul in Romans xvi. 10. It should be added that, according to some legends, Aristobulus died in the year 99, and was buried at Glastonbury. Welsh traditions say that Arwystli Hên (Aristobulus the old) accompanied the family of Caradog (Caractacus) on their return to Britain ; see the History of Wales, by Jane Williams, pp. 29 and 41, where numerous references are given ; cf. Ussher's Brit. Eccl. Antiq. (otherwise called Ussher's Primordia), p. 9. The notion that the first missionary to Britain was, however, no other than St Joseph himself, is stoutly maintained by Broughton, in his Ecclesiastical Historie of Great Britaine, 1633. He cites many authorities and has said nearly all that can be said in support of the legend. The headings of some of his chapters will sufficiently indicate his conclusions.

" Age i. ch. xxi. Of the coming of S. Joseph of Aramathia, who buryed Christ, into this our Britaine ; And how it is made doubtfull, or denyed by many writers, but without either reason or Authoritie."

[1] From "The Origin of the English Nation," by E. A. Freeman, in Macmillan's Magazine, May, 1870, p. 41.

[2] Note by Sir T. Duffus Hardy in his edition of William of Malmesbury.

"Ch. xxii. Wherein is proved by all kinde of testimonies, and authorities, that for certaine, S. Joseph of Aramathia, with diuers other holy Associates, came into, preached, lyued, dyed, and was buryed in Britayne, at the place now called Glastenbury in Summersetshire." . . .

"Ch. xxv. That many other Christians came hither, especially into the Northren parts, and Ilands, with S. Joseph of Aramathia, besides them which continued with him at Glastenbury; and many of them married with Britans continuing Christianitie heare in their children and posteritie, vntill the generall Conuersion of Britaine, vnder the first Christian Kings, Lucius, & Donaldus."

He does not omit to mention the miraculous trees, and he expresses himself much to the same effect in his "Monastichon Britanicum," 1655, and in his "True Memorial of the Ancient, most holy, and Religious State of Great Britain," 1650; which two books differ in nothing but their title-page.

On the whole, I see no great difficulty in believing that some Christian missionaries had arrived in Britain, and that a rude kind of chapel had been erected at Glastonbury, before the close of the second century, or even fifty years earlier; but it must be confessed that the statements concerning this early introduction of Christianity into Britain are all alike vague, spurious, or insufficient. The only way to arrive at the truth is by collecting all the early statements on the subject, and by tabulating them according to their value. This has been done most completely and carefully by Mr Haddan, in Appendix A to the "Councils and Ecclesiastical Documents relating to Great Britain and Ireland," edited by A. W. Haddan and W. Stubbs, vol. i. 1869. He shews that there is no historical evidence for the existence of Christians in Britain earlier than that of Tertullian (adv. Jud. vii.), which only carries us back to about A.D. 200. By a careful analysis, he proves that "Statements respecting (α) British Christians at Rome, (β) British Christians in Britain, (γ) Apostles or Apostolic men preaching in Britain in the *First Century*, rest upon either guess, mistake, or fable;" and again, that "Evidence alleged for the existence of a Christian Church in Britain during the *Second Century* is similarly unhistorical." With these incontrovertible results we must rest contented. The various legends evidently arose from the wish to claim for Britain some one person at least who is mentioned in Holy Scripture, and hence we find such claims advanced for St Peter, St Paul, James the son of Zebedee, and Simon Zelotes; whilst other writers, perhaps thinking these notions too ambitious, were contented with the names of St Joseph, Aristobulus, or even the Claudia mentioned by St Paul in 2 Tim. iv. 21. All such accounts are alike fabulous, and the names of Britain's first missionaries must ever remain unknown; whilst we can hardly approximate more closely to the date of their arrival than by the vague statement, that it was before the year 208.

§ 13. JOSEPH OF ARIMATHEA.

In examining the account of Joseph of Arimathea as related by John of Glastonbury, we at once find that it is separable into two distinct parts, the one of which is *legendary* and does not greatly transgress the bounds of probability, whilst the other part is purely *fabulous* and obviously of later invention.[1] For the purpose of making this distinction, the account of William of Malmesbury is most valuable, and altogether to be relied on. He tells us how St Joseph was sent over by St Philip, and how a king of Britain, whom he does not name, gave Joseph and his companions the island called Ynyswitryn, where, by admonition of the Archangel Gabriel appearing to him in a vision, he built a chapel which he dedicated to the Virgin. After which two other kings, whom again he does not name, gave the twelve holy men the Twelve Hides of Glastonbury. Later still, the place where so many holy men had lived became for a short time a lurking-place for wild beasts. He afterwards adds a few marvels; such as the piercing of St David's hand, an account of a crucifix that spoke, of another from which the crown fell down, and of another from which blood flowed when the figure of Christ was wounded by an arrow. He also briefly refers to Arthur. But the points about which he seems to have known nothing are these. He does not make any reference to the Assumption of the Virgin; he knows nothing of Joseph's son Josephe, nothing of Josephes'

---

[1] Both parts are alike untrue, but I think my meaning is clear. Many old writers who accepted the part of the story which rested on ecclesiastical tradition rejected that which rested only on romances.

consecration at Sarras, nothing about the extraordinary story of the
pilgrims crossing the sea on Josephes' shirt, nor has he a word about
king Mordrains. He omits the four verses at the bottom of p. 69,
where Josephes is again mentioned; and he makes no allusion to
the Graal, or to Lancelot or Gawain, or to the prophecy of Melkin;
all of which is just what we should expect. Of the purely fabulous
part of the story, of all that relates to Josephes, Mordrains, and Sarras, he gives no indication; and his silence about Joseph bringing any
holy relics with him is very significant.[1] It is true that in speaking
of Arthur he speaks slightingly of the trifling fables of the Britons
concerning him (Will. Malm. ed. T. D. Hardy, i. 14); but it does
not follow that he would wittingly omit a strange legend about a
saint. Again, it has been remarked that Geoffrey of Monmouth
does not say one word about Joseph of Arimathea; and yet he has
plenty to say about Merlin. I believe the true and simple explanation of this to be that what I have called the *fabulous* portion of
this narrative was not invented till after the death of Geoffrey, which
took place in 1154. The *legendary* portion was probably known
centuries earlier, as seems to be shown by the quarrel between St
Augustine and the Britons, "who preferred their own traditions
before all the churches in the world" (Beda's Eccl. Hist. Bk. ii. ch.
2; cf. Montalembert, Monks of the West, vol. iii. p. 25 (translation);
Paulin Paris, Romans de la Table Ronde, i. 95). The fullest form
of the legend—but one unconnected with Britain—known in early
times, is that contained in the Apocryphal Gospel of Nicodemus and
similar writings, which tell us how Joseph was imprisoned by the
Jews, but miraculously delivered by Christ, who appeared to him in
the prison, shewed him the Tomb in which Himself had been laid
by the saint's pious care, and then, taking him by the hand, set
him in his own city of Arimathea. See Cowper's Apocryphal Gospels, pp. 249, 259, 290, 296, 332, 341, 428, &c. A translation of

[1] In the excellently written account of the Legend of St Joseph in the
Acta Sanctorum (xvii Martii), the writer is incredulous about St Joseph's
coming to Britain, and says he believes that this story must have been invented
by the writer of the Romance of the Graal; but he seems to have entirely
overlooked the account in William of Malmesbury; which makes a good deal
of difference as regards the latter part of the statement.

one of these accounts exists in Anglo-Saxon (MS. Camb. Univ. Lib.
Ii. 2. 11), and has been edited by Thwaites. The story of Joseph's
imprisonment occurs also in Gregory of Tours, who died about A.D.
595; seé Gregorii Turonensis, Hist. Francorum, lib. i. cap. xx,
printed by Migne. But to the *fabulous* portion of the story, in which
the Grail is mentioned, there is only *one* reference involving a date
earlier than the twelfth century; and a very extraordinary passage
it is. Helinand, a Cistercian monk in the Abbey of Froidmond in
the diocese of Beauvais, who died about A.D. 1219 or 1223, wrote a
chronicle ending with the year 1209, in which he has a very curious
entry under the date A.D. 717. The passage has been quoted by
Vincent of Beauvais, in his Speculum Historiale, and by John of
Tynemouth, in his Historia Aurea; the original passage is printed in
vol. 212 of Migne's Cursus Patrologiæ, and is cited by M. Paulin
Paris, Romans de la Table Ronde, tom. i. p. 91. I prefer to quote
it from a MS. of John of Tynemouth (Camb. Univ. Libr. Dd. 10.
22, fol. 10 *b*), which omits the words *cum suo jure*, i. e. "together
with their gravy," after *dapes*, but has the inserted clause—*gradatim,
vnus morsellus post alium in diuersis ordinibus.*

" De Ioseph centurione, ca^m. 4.

Hoc tempore in britannia cuidam heremite demonstrata fuit mirabilis quedam visio per angelum de Ioseph decurione nobili, qui
corpus domini deposuit de cruce, & de catino illo vel parapside in quo
dominus cenauit cum discipulis suis; de quo ab eodem heremita
descripta est historia que dicitur gradale. Gradalis autem vel gradale
gallice dicitur scutella lata & aliquantulum profunda, in qua preciose
dapes diuitibus solent apponi gradatim, vnus morsellus post alium in
diuersis ordinibus. Dicitur & vulgari nomine graal, quia grata et acceptabilis est in ea comedenti, tum propter continens, quia forte
argentea est vel de alia preciosa materia, tum propter contentum .i.
ordinem multiplicem dapium preciosarum. Hanc historiam latine
scriptam inuenire non potui set tantum gallice scripta habetur a
quibusdam proceribus, nec facile vt aiunt tota inueniri potest."

The question is simply, is the date 717 genuine, or fictitious ?
I cannot believe it to be genuine, but think it to be purely the invention of Walter Map; for the French prose romance of the Seynt
Graal gives the identical daté 717 as the year when the book of the
Graal was written by a purely imaginary hermit; see the "Seynt

Graal," ed. F. J. Furnivall, p. 1. Yet, if I understand him rightly, M. Paulin Paris, the best authority on this matter, accepts the date as in a measure genuine, in the sense that some old traditions concerning the Graal were about that time cherished by the Britons with a peculiar interest. I think Mr Morley's opinion to be here the more correct, when he says that "Helinand testifies to the immediate acceptance of the legendary origin ascribed artistically to Map's tale of the Graal, by actually placing under the year 707 [read 717] the introductory story of the vision that appeared to a certain hermit in Britain, of St Joseph and the Graal," &c.; Morley's English Writers, vol. i. p. 568. It is clear that the passage only proves that the French prose romance of the Graal (which probably had a Latin original) was written before 1209. It would take up far too much space to consider all the numerous points of interest connected with the origin of the Graal legends. The subject is most carefully treated by M. Paulin Paris; and again, an excellent account of them is given by Professor Morley, in his English Writers, vol. i. pp. 562—573. Only lately, Dr F. G. Bergmann has issued an inexpensive pamphlet entitled "The San Grëal; an inquiry into the origin and signification of the Romances of the San Grëal," which, if not always accurate, is at any rate well worth reading. I can only state some of the results to which these and other books lead. Dr Bergmann mentions five authors as especially to be noted as writers of Graal Romances, viz. Guiot le Provençal, Chrestien de Troyes, Walter Map (commonly called Mapes), Wolfram von Eschenbach, and Albrecht von Scharfenberg. He claims "the glory of having invented the Grëal" for the first of these, viz. Guiot. But the proof is doubtful, for the work of Guiot has perished, and all that we know about him is derived from the scanty data furnished by his German imitator, Wolfram, who did not begin his poem till 1204. Again, the "Lancelot" of Chrestien de Troyes has been proved conclusively by a Flemish scholar, W. J. A. Jonckbloet, to have been founded upon the "Lancelot" of Walter Map; and in like manner I suppose that Chrestien borrowed his "Percival le Gallois" from Map also, in a great measure. Wolfram and Albrecht certainly wrote later than Map, and I can see no reason why we may not assume Walter

Map's romance, of which the original Latin version is lost, to have been the real original from which all the rest were more or less imitated. This is Professor Morley's conclusion, who very pertinently asks—" Where was there an author able to invent it and to write it with a talent so 'prodigious,' except Walter Map, to whom alone, and to whom always positively, it has been ascribed ? " The extraordinary genius of this great writer is sufficiently evinced by the works of his which are still extant. If we put the date of Geoffrey of Monmouth's history at 1145—1147, and suppose that Walter Map wrote his first Romance, viz. " Joseph," at least twenty years after the appearance of Geoffrey of Monmouth's history (Morley's Eng. Writ. i. 563), we get the approximate date of its composition to be 1170, or probably, as it seems to me, a few years earlier.

§ 14. The original Latin text by Walter Map being lost, we are left to conjecture what it was like from the various translations and imitations of it. And first, there is the Romance in French verse, as composed by Robert de Boron about A.D. 1170. This exists only in one MS., No. 1987 in the Bibliothèque Impériale at Paris. It was first printed by M. Michel in 1841, and has been reprinted by Mr Furnivall in his " Seynt Graal," edited for the Roxburghe Club in 1861. It is not quite perfect, having a gap in the middle of the story. An analysis of the contents is given by M. Paulin Paris, " Les Romans de la Table Ronde," i. 123. Secondly, there is a French prose rendering of this same version, extant in an unprinted MS. now in the possession of Mr Huth, of which some account was given in " The Athenæum," Dec. 11, 1869. There is a great deal of similarity in the language of these two versions, shewing that one is immediately derived from the other. Compare, for instance, the following passage from the Huth MS. (fol. 15)—

" cil de cele compaignie parlerent ensamble & disent. que il auoient pitie de moys. & dient que il emprieront yoseph. Et vinrent tout ensamble a lui. & se laissierent chaoir [deuant] ses pies & li priierent tout ensamble mierchi. Et yoseph sermeruilla moult & dist. Que voles vous. Et il dient a yoseph. Li plus des gens qui vinrent chi sen sont ale por chou que nous eusmes la grasce de cel graal,"[1] &c.—

---

[1] I cannot answer for the correctness of the spelling, having only seen a transcript of the MS., not the MS. itself.

with the corresponding passage in the verse copy (p. 32, col. 1, in Mr Furnivall's Seynt Graal, vol. i. appendix),

> " *De Moyses leur prist pité,*
> *Et dirent* qu'il en palleroient
> A Joseph et *l'en pricroient.*
> *Quant tout ensemble Joseph virent,*
> *Trestout devant ses piez chéirent,*
> *Et li prie* chaucuns et breit
> Qu'il de Moyset pitié eit ;
> *Et Joseph mout se merveilla*
> De ce que chascuns le pria,
> Et leur ha *dist : Vous, que voulez ?*
> Dites-moi de quoi vous priez."
> Il respondent hisnelement :
> " *Li plus granz* feis de nostre *gent*
> *S'en sunt alé* et departi ;
> Un seul en ha demouré ci
> Qui pleure mout très tenrement,
> Et crie et fait grant marrement,
> Et dist que il ne s'en ira
> De ce tant comm' il vivera.
> Il nous prie que te prions,
> De la grace que nous avuns," &c.

This passage also shews that the above-mentioned prose version is more compressed ; but it is not easy to say whether it is epitomized from the verse copy, or the latter expanded from the former.

Thirdly, there is the *long* French prose version, in which the whole story is much expanded and considerably altered, existing in several MSS., and printed in Mr Furnivall's " Seynt Graal " from MS. Bibl. Reg. xiv. E. iii. in the British Museum, with some readings from MS. Addit. 10292.

The English Alliterative Poem is a condensed version from the third and longest of these three versions; hence the frequent references to Mr Furnivall's " Seynt Graal " in my notes. The prefaces to this work, by Mr Furnivall and Herr Schulz, should be consulted.

Mr Furnivall's book further contains an English rimed version made by Henry Lonelich, in the time of Henry VI. This is of great length, and follows the long French prose version tolerably closely. It is spoken of by Warton, Hist. Eng. Poetry, ed. 1840, vol. i. p. 149. The MS. is in Corpus Christi College, Cambridge, No. 80.

I may here quote a useful passage in Herr Schulz's Essay (Seynt Graal, i. p. xv). He omits to mention Walter Map and Robert de Boron.

"The oldest narrator of these histories, and who is at the same time known by name, is Chrestiens de Troyes, in his *Li Contes del Graal*.[1] He left this MS. in an incomplete state, and the MSS. of his work are mentioned to us in their order by three continuators of the work—Gautiers de Dinet, Gerbers, and Manestiers.

"Another treatment of the same matter, in the main, by a North French Poet, probably a contemporary of Chrestiens de Troyes, is afforded by the MS. at Berne, entitled *Percheval le Galois*, on which Rochat reports *in extenso*,[2] and where, at pp. 165 and 176, he gives, as his result, that this work, in spite of many coincidences, does *not* emanate from Chrestiens de Troyes.

"A third version of the Graal- and Percival-sagas was furnished to us Germans by Wolfram von Eschenbach, in his *Parcival* (composed from about 1204 to 1210).[3] In it he followed a French poet, Kyot [Guiot] of Provence, a Provençal who, however, wrote in Northern French, as it was spoken in Champagne, the only dialect which Wolfram von Eschenbach understood. As Kyot's French poem has unfortunately not hitherto been discovered, it is impossible to determine what measure of liberty Wolfram has taken in his version of Kyot's works; but his *Titurel*-fragments, which stand in the closest connection with the 'Parcival,' prove that Kyot must have narrated numerous adventures, which Wolfram, for the purpose of more completely rounding off the Graal and Parcival stories, omitted from his romance, and which still afforded abundant material for a second tale, namely, of the *Tschianatulander* and *Sigune*, which Wolfram, however, unfortunately left incomplete, and of which those two so-called *Titurel*-fragments form only a small part.

"The above-mentioned omitting of many adventures narrated by Kyot, is confirmed by the German *Later Titurel*,[4] by a poet of the

---

[1] About him, consult W. L. Holland, "Chrestiens de Troyes;" Tübingen, Fues. 1854, pp. 195—225; where many books on the subject are mentioned.

[2] A. Rochat. On a hitherto unknown "Percheval le Galois;" Zürich, Kiesling, 1855.

[3] The original text, edited by Lachmann, was published at Berlin by Reimer, 1833. Translated, with an Introduction and explanations, by San Marte (A. Schulz), 2nd edition, Leipsic, Brockhaus, 1858. Likewise translated by Simrock, Stuttgart and Tübingen; Cotta, new edition, 1858. [A brief analysis, in English, is given in Bergmann's San Grëal.]

[4] First printed in 1477. Modern edition by K. A. Hahn. Titurel: Quedlinburg and Leipsic, Basse, 1842. See an extensive extract, with notes,

name of Albrecht, whose composition comes at the end of the 13th century. He also refers to Kyot the Provençal, but adds the history of the final pilgrimage of the Graal to the East, into the realm of Prester John.[1] It is a matter of doubt, however, whether he ever saw Kyot's original work; and the probability is, that he took the subject-matter from other poems based upon Kyot, and which are unknown to us."

In the "Seynt Graal," pref. p. vii, it is shewn, by Mr W. D. Nash, that the story is not of British origin, as relates to the Graal at least. At p. 3 of the text, the date already mentioned (A.D. 717) is given as the time when the story was first revealed to a certain hermit; and an astonishing assertion is elsewhere made, that the Latin book, the true original, was written by no mortal hand. I forbear to quote the blasphemy further; we may acquit Walter Map, I hope, of daring to originate such a lie himself.

§ 15. The above account may suffice. Further information is to be obtained from the authors quoted, especially from M. Paulin Paris, Mr Morley, and Mr Furnivall. I will only recapitulate the chief points. Dividing the History of Joseph into its legendary and fabulous portions by the criterion furnished us by William of Malmesbury, the former part is again subdivisible into two portions; viz. the legend of Joseph's imprisonment, as related in the Gospel of Nicodemus, the Acts of Pilate, and other early Eastern apocryphal writings, and secondly, the legend of his arrival in England, which was firmly believed in at Glastonbury at an early period. Next there is the account connected with the date 717, which was certainly a later invention. Lastly, the fabulous portion of the story bursts suddenly into full vigour, and is spread abroad by Walter Map, by Robert de Boron, Guyot le Provençal, and Chrestien de Troyes with wonderful rapidity, and at much about the same time, viz. about A.D. 1170. How far any of these was indebted to the other, it is hard to say. Robert de Boron does not pretend to much originality.[2]

and an "Essay on the Graal-Saga," in San Marte's "Life and Poems of Wolfram von Eschenbach," vol. ii. p. 86—294, and 361—453.

On the ground of the Epistola Johannis Presbyteri, missa ad Gubernatorem Constantinopolitanum, in Assemanni Bibliotheca Orientalis, tom. iii. pt. ii. p. 490; published Romæ, 1728.

[2] I am much puzzled by M. Paulin Paris's statement, tom. i. p. 106. From a certain passage he seems to infer that Robert de Boron had *not* before his

§ 16. ON THE WORD "GRAAL."

This word, very frequently used *without* the prefix *Seynt, Seint, Saint, Sainct,* or *San* in the earlier copies, is variously spelt *Graal, Greal, Graaus, Grasal,* or *Grazal* in Norman-French, *Grasal, Grazal,* or *Grazaus* in Provençal, *Grisal* in Old Catalan, and *Grial* in Old Spanish. In modern French, it is written *Graal, Grëal,* and *Gréal;* in Old English it is *Graile* or *Grayle,* as e. g. in Spenser, F. Q. bk. ii. c. x. st. 53—

" Yet true it is, that long before that day
Hither came Joseph of Arimathy,
Who brought with him the *holy grayle,* they say,
And preacht the truth ; but since it greatly did decay."

Mr Wedgwood's account of the word is as follows ; (Etym. Dict. ii. 171). "Languedoc *grazal, grezal,* a large earthen dish or bowl, bassin de terre de *grès. Grais, grez,* [is] potter's earth, freestone. Provençal *grasal, grazal,* 'un *grasal* ou jatte pleine de prunes.'—Raynouard. *Grais* or *grès* seems the Latinized form of the Breton *krâg,* hard stone ; *eur pôd krâg,* un pot de *grès.* So Norse *gryta,* a pot, from *griot,* stone." Elsewhere, viz. s. v. Grit, he explains the Fr. *grès* by gritty stone ; and considers it cognate with the German and Dutch *gries,* and the English *grit,* A.S. *greot.* A similar derivation is given by Borel. But the derivation suggested by Roquefort, and strongly supported by Burguy and M. Paulin Paris, is decidedly preferable. Roquefort shews conclusively that the dish called *greal* was used at great feasts and was of costly material (cf. the extract from Helinand above, p. xxx), and therefore not of earth or stone. The word is, in fact, the Low Latin *gradale* or *grasale,* which occurs in Ducange or in Charpentier's Supplement in the very numerous forms *gradale, gradalus, grasala, grasale, grayale, grassale, grazala, grassala,* with the diminutives *gradella, gracellus, grassella, grasilhia, grassellus,* and *grasaletus !* Charpentier further tells us that the signification is—a kind of vessel, of wood, earth, or metal, and not always implying the same notion ; for it occurs both

eyes the Latin original. From the same passage (l. 929, p. 11, of Appendix to "Seynt Graal"), I infer the exact contrary.

in the sense of a large, round, and shallow vessel, Fr. *jatte* [a bowl], and also " pro *lancis* seu *catini* specie" for the use of the table, Fr. *plat* [a dish]. All the above forms are various corruptions from a diminutive *cratella* of the Latin *crater* or *cratera*, which again is from the Greek κρατήρ or κρατηρία, a bowl in which things could be mixed up. In a precisely similar manner the modern French *grille* is formed from the Latin *craticula*, the diminutive of *crates*. M. Paulin aptly cites the Fr. *gras* from the Lat. *crassus* to shew the initial change, and O. Fr. *paelle* from the Lat. *patella*, to illustrate the loss of the *t*. At any rate, it is certain that the original sense of *graal* was a bowl, or dish, and the *seynt graal* was that Holy Dish which was used at the Last Supper, stolen by a servant of Pilate—so says the story,—used by Pilate to wash his hands in before the multitude, given by Pilate to Joseph as a memorial of Christ, and finally used by Joseph to collect the Holy Blood flowing from the five wounds. But of course it was soon seen by the romance-writers that this first idea was a mistake. The Vessel containing the Blood should rather have been the Cup, and this alteration was soon made. Even Robert de Boron tells us that the true *spiritual* meaning of the Graal was, that it signified the Holy Chalice. Christ is made to appear in a vision, and declare this explicitly to Joseph, in ll. 907—910 of the early French verse; see Seynt Graal, Appendix,

> " Cist viessiaus ou men sanc meis,
> Quant de men cors le requeillis,
> Calices apelez sara."

That is, " this Vessel, in which thou didst put My Blood when thou didst collect it from My Body, shall be called the Chalice." [1]

This idea prevailed more and more, until the two words *san greal*, having lost their original meaning, were turned into *sang real*, and interpreted by *real blood;* an explanation which is actually given by Ménage as the true one, and believed in by many at the present day! It deserves to be mentioned, however, that the translation *real blood* is rather a lame one, as the usual meaning of the

---

[1] Hence the expression in Tennyson's " Holy Grail," p. 36—
 " The cup, the cup itself, from which our Lord
 Drank at the last sad supper with his own."

O. Fr. *real* is *royal*. And in fact, the combination *sank real* actually occurs in Old English in the signification of *royal blood ;* as, e. g. in l. 179 of Morte Arthure (ed. Perry, E. E. T. S.) p. 6, where it is spelt *saunke realle*. Only 4 lines above, in l. 175, the Romans are said to be "of þe realeste blode" (i. e. "the most royal blood") upon earth. Skelton says, moreover, that Cardinal Wolsey

—"came of the *sank royall*
That was cast out of a bochers stall."
Why Come Ye Nat To Courte ? l. 490.

But this interpretation—*real blood*—is not the only false interpretation. The old romance-writers, who wrote whilst the *g* still always belonged to the second word, were driven to account for the word *greal* by deriving it from *grè*, i. e. from the Latin *gratus*, pleasing. Accordingly, they gravely tell us that the *greal* is so called because it is so *agreeable*. This explanation is given in the extract above, p. xxx., in the Huth MS. fol. 14 *b*, and in Robert de Boron's version ; see Seynt Graal, vol. i. Appendix, p. 31. The fact that the early writers were driven to such a shift as this very sufficiently disposes of the late derivation suggested by Ménage.

§ 17. But the difficulties connected with the word do not end here. Besides the Low-Latin *gradale*, a bowl, there is another Low-Latin *gradale* with another meaning. This *gradale* is a variation of *graduale*, the service-book or Antiphonary for High Mass, containing the portions to be sung by the Choir, and so called from certain phrases which were sung, after the Epistle, *in gradibus*, upon the steps of the choir, as directed in the rubric in the Sarum Missal. "Quando epistola legitur, duo pueri in superpelliceis, facta inclinatione ad altare *ante gradum chori* in pulpitum per medium chori ad *Gradale* incipiendum se præparent, et suum versum cantandum." See Procter, on the Common Prayer, 3rd ed. 1857, pp. 8 and 317. As might be expected, this word *gradale* also assumes the form *graile* or *grayle* in Early English,[1] as in the Promptorium Parvulorum, where we find the entry—"*Grayle*, boke. *Gradale, vel*

---

[1] It even takes the form *grasal* in Old French ; see the note in M. Paulin Paris ; Les Romans, &c. tom. i. p. 379. The form *grazal* is given by Ducange.

gradalis," upon which see Mr Way's note. Mr Way concludes by telling us that the statute 3 and 4 Edw. VI. for abolishing divers books and images, enacts "that all books called antiphoners, missals, *grails*, processionals, &c. heeretofore used for service of the church, shall be cleerelie and vtterlie abolished, and forbidden for euer to be vsed or kept in this realme."[1] The question may arise, were these two uses of the O. Fr. *grael* ever confused? M. Paris assumes that they were, and that the story of the Holy Graal was originally inserted in a *Gradale* by a Welsh clerk about A.D. 717. I am not convinced by this explanation, nor am I persuaded that it can be evolved from the opening passage of the long French prose romance. It is, however, quite true that the name *graal* was applied to the romance itself, as well as to the vessel, as e. g. in the lines—

> " Issi nus counte le Graal,
> Le lyvre de la seint vassal "—

which occur in the History of Fulk fitz-warine, ed. Wright, Warton Club, 1855; p. 181.

Nor are the meanings of the word even yet exhausted. The Lat. *graculus*, a jackdaw, produced the O. Fr. *graille*, from which was formed *grailler*, to cry like a jackdaw, also to recall dogs with a horn. The Lat. *craticula* produced the O. Fr. *grail*, now spelt *grille*. The Lat. *gracilis* produced the O. Fr. *graile* or *gresle*, fine, small, delicate, which was also used as a substantive to signify a shrill-sounding musical instrument. Hence Mr Park may be not far wrong when he interprets *in graile* by "in small particles" in the quotation made by Nares from Ritson's Songs, vol. ii, p. 64—

> " Nor yet the delight, that comes to the sight
> To see how it [the ale] flowers and mantles *in graile*."

If we here take *in graile* to refer to *very fine* beads or air-bubbles, we probably get the true sense. And hence, again, we find *grails* used to mean the fine or small feathers of a hawk ; see Halliwell. Lastly, from the O. Fr. *gres*, mod. Fr. *grès*, which is our Eng. *grit*, comes the O. Fr. *gresle*, mod. Fr. *grêle*, hail, and the mod. F. *grésil*, sleet. Hence the prov. Eng. *grailing*, a slight fall of hail, just

---

[1] See other examples in Nares, s. v. *Graile*.

enough to cover the ground, in Halliwell; and the word *graile*, used by Spenser to signify fine gravel, F. Q. bk. i. c. vii. st. 6. But it is clear that the O. Fr. *gresle*, fine, and *gresle*, hail, with their derivatives, may easily have been confused with each other.

§ 18. As regards the Holy Vessel itself, the legends tell us that it was finally transported to India, and still remains there. Nevertheless, at the capture of Cæsarea [1] in 1101, the Crusaders found what they imagined to be the very Dish itself, made of one large emerald. It was sent to Genoa, and there shewn as a relic, till Napoleon I. transported it to Paris. In 1815 it was sent back to Genoa, but was cracked in the journey. At Genoa it is still preserved, in the treasury of the Cathedral of San Lorenzo, and is still venerated as being the veritable *Sacro Catino*. It is really made of greenish glass, and of an hexagonal shape. It may be seen by the curious, and is duly noted as being one of the curiosities of Genoa in Murray's Handbook to North Italy, p. 106. For further description of it, see Nares's Glossary, s. v. *Graal*. This is not the only one, however; for Dr Bergmann says that one was sent by the patriarch of Jerusalem to Henry III. of England in 1247, and that another one once existed at Constantinople. The book of Melkin tells us that Joseph did not bring a Dish to England, but two sacred cruets, viz. those delineated at p. 35. These were buried at Glastonbury, and will be found whenever the sarcophagus of Joseph is found ; after which there will never again be a drought in England. It is almost worth while, then, to look for them !

§ 19. As regards the symbolical meaning of the myth involved in the Graal legend, the connection between the tale of Pheredur in the "Red Book" and the Romance of Percival, the relation of the Graal itself to Ceridwen's cauldron and the ancient Druidic rites, I must refer the reader to the Essay on "The Sangreal" in the second series of S. Baring Gould's "Curious Myths of the Middle Ages." And I here take the opportunity to observe that those who take up my edition of The Romans of Partenay (E. E. T. S., 1866) should

---

[1] Roquefort (s. v. *Graal*) quotes an account from the Chroniques de Loys xii, by Jehan d'Autun, which gives the same date, but speaks of the capture of *Jerusalem*. But Jerusalem was taken A.D. 1099.

read the Essay, in the same volume, upon "Melusina;" whilst a third Essay, entitled "The Knight of the Swan," well illustrates Mr Gibbs's edition of the Cheuelere Assigne (E. E. T. S., Extra Series, 1868). The religious signification of the Grail-legend in its relation to Christianity is considered by M. Fauriel, in his "Histoire de la Poésie Provençale," tom. ii. chap. 26 and 27.

§ 20. EVALAK'S SHIELD; ARGENT, A CROSS, GULES.

The shield given to Evalak by Josaphe, son of Joseph of Arimathea, plays a considerable part in our Alliterative Poem. Besides which, the Story of Joseph was recounted to Galahad by the White Knight solely for the sake of accounting for this shield. After Evalak's victory over Tholomer, the red cross upon it vanished; but we read that Josaphes, just before his death, bade Mordrains bring the shield to him; after which he (Josaphes) bled at the nose, made a cross upon the shield with his blood, and gave it again to Mordrains. Subsequently it was placed upon duke Nasciens' tomb, to be left there till Galahad should come and take it. Galahad was afterwards so fortunate as to obtain also a sword which had belonged to king David, the hilt of which had been covered by Solomon with precious stones. We then come to his adventure with the holy bleeding lance, his achievement of the Saint Graal, and his death at Sarras. See Malory's Morte Darthur, bk. xvii. We find a similar account, with some slight variations, in Hardyng's Chronicle, edited by Sir H. Ellis, 1812. Hardyng professes to follow "Mewyn, the Britayn chronicler," who is probably no other than Melkin, of whose book it would be interesting to know somewhat more than is told us by him and John of Glastonbury. A few extracts from Hardyng may be not out of place here.

Chap. xlvii. of his Chronicle relates "how Ioseph Aramathie came vnto Britayne with Vaspasyan, and chrystened a part of this lande."

In Chap. xlviij, we have the account "howe Ioseph conuerted this kyng Aruiragus, & gaue hym a shelde of yᵉ armes that wee call sainct George his armes, whiche armes he bare euer after; & thus became that armes to bee yᵉ kynges armes of this lande, long afore sainct George was gotten or borne. And as Maryan, the profounde

chronicler, saieth, he bare of siluer, in token of clennes, a crosse of
goules, [in] significacion of the bloodde that Christe bleedde on y⁰
crosse, and for it muste nedes of reason be called a crosse.

> IOseph conuerted this kyng Aruigarus,
> By his prechyng, to knowe y⁰ lawe deuine,
> And baptized hym, as writen hath Mewinus,[1]
> The chronicler, in Bretain tongue full fyne,
> And to Christe[s] lawe made hym enclyne ;
> And gaue hym then a shelde of siluer white,
> A crosse endlong and ouerthwart full perfect," &c.

In Chapter lxxvii, we have an account of the achievement of the
Sege Perilous by Galahad—

> "Whiche Joseph sayd afore that tyme ful long,
> In Mewyns booke, the Britayn chronicler,
> As writen is the Britons iestes emong,
> That Galaad the knight, and virgyne clere
> Shuld it acheue and auentures all in fere
> Of the seynt Graale, and of the great Briteyn,
> And afterwarde a virgyne dye certeyne."

He next gees on to tell how Galaad came to Auelon, and found
there a white shield bearing a red cross, a shield, and a spear, the
shield having been left there by Joseph, and the sword by Naciens.
Four years afterwards, Galaad finds the Saint Graal in Wales, after
which he goes to Sarras and is made king of Sarras—

> Where thenne he made .xij. knightes of the order
> Of saynt Graall, in full signifycacyon
> Of the table [of] whiche Ioseph was the founder,
> At Aualon, as Mewyn made relacyon ;
> In token of the table and refyguracyon
> Of the brotherhede of Christes souper & maundie
> Afore his death, of hyghest dignytee."

Galaad dies at Sarras, says Hardyng, but sends Percival with his
heart to Arthur, praying the king to bury the heart beside king
Evalak and duke Seraphe, who were buried beside Joseph in the
chapel of Our Lady at Glastonbury. This was done, and the
famous shield was hung over Galaad's heart's tomb. And this is the
last that we hear of it. A like "silver shielde," with "a bloudie
Crosse" scored upon it, forms part of the armour of the Red-Cross

---

[1] Other readings *Nenius, Neninus ;* but *Melkin* is probably meant ; see
note above, p. xxi.

Knight, St George, as described by Spenser in the opening stanzas of the Faerie Queene. St George, however, was not considered as the *special* patron of England till after the siege of Calais in 1349. The banner of St George, white with a red cross, floated beside that of the Austrian empire a century earlier, in 1245; see "Curious Myths," &c., by S. Baring Gould, 2nd Series, p. 49, 2nd edition. A century earlier still, in 1146, the white standard, with the blood-red cross, was borne by the Knights Templars, having been granted to them by Pope Eugenius III. The white ground denoted chastity, and the red cross was the symbol of martyrdom. See "The Knights Templars," by C. G. Addison, 3rd ed. 1852, pp. 25, 26. The earliest mention of the red cross as a badge is in the speech of Pope Urban II. in 1094—" wear it, a red, a bloody cross, as an external mark, on your breasts or shoulders ;" Gibbon, Decline and Fall, ch. lviii. Further researches concerning the Red Cross soon involve us in the mysteries of the Rosicrucians, concerning whom it may suffice to refer the reader to a late work on the subject, by Hargrave Jennings. I little thought, when writing the above remarks, that, before the proofsheets of this preface could be corrected, the RED CROSS would be floating, an emblem of Mercy, over French and German ambulances.

The Knights Templars, the Brethren of the Order of the Temple of Solomon at Jerusalem, are first heard of in 1118. Their vows and their principle of association strongly remind us of the knights of romance, who engaged in the quest of the Saint Graal. Indeed Herr Schulz tells us expressly (Seynt Graal, vol. i. p. xx) that Wolfram von Eschenbach, in his *Parcival*, gives the name of *Templeisen* (Fr. *Les Templiers*) to the guardians of the Holy Vessel.

§ 21. REMARKS.

Before concluding this Preface, I must express my sincere thanks to Mr Furnivall for various useful suggestions and for his loan of a transcript of the Huth MS., and to Dr Morris for some notes upon difficult and unusual words. Mr Parker and Mr Brock have also rendered me much help.

Whilst engaged on editing the pieces in this book, some points have suggested themselves to me which I here put down as briefly as possible.

The legend of the Graal was added to and altered so often that I do not think we ought to expect that any one leading idea was kept always in view. In many cases, mere invention of new incidents seems to be all that the compilers thought of. To regard the series of legends as a whole, and to find that they always embody some central thought is just what we moderns are so prone to do ; but it may be doubted whether the writers of them would not be very much astonished at such a proceeding. For instance, given the existence of a Saint Graal, which only a few knights could hope to see, the romance of the Queste of the Saint Graal *follows* naturally ; but the Queste may have been an after-thought, for all that.

The series seems to have begun with the story of Joseph for no other reason than that he was the great British saint, and was moreover said to have been buried at Glastonbury, where king Arthur was buried also. Hence the idea of introducing the story of Arthur by a romance concerning Joseph arose naturally enough.

It being once resolved upon to make Joseph the subject of a romance, the notion of a holy dish containing Christ's blood starts up at once. It is his natural symbol, just as St Catharine has her wheel, and St Sebastian his arrow. His other symbol, to signify the great distance over which he had travelled, was of course a staff. Out of this staff *grew*, in the most literal sense, the miraculous thorn and the wonderful walnut-tree ; and, later still, the thorn-tree became three thorn-trees.

The great excitement of the middle of the twelfth century was the second crusade, begun in 1146. A little earlier, the order of the Knights Templars had been established. This was a *fighting* order of Knights, quite unlike that of the Knights of St John. Their object was religious glory, and their destination the East. How exactly all this is reproduced in the history of the Knights of the Round Table, seeking a holy object, and finding it likewise in the East ! Godfrey de Bouillon, king of Jerusalem, meets with the success of Evalak, king of Sarras. Galahad's shield bears the Templars' device. The Saracens were then frequently heard of ; hence Joseph goes to Sarras, their supposed city. The conversion of the people of Sarras is an artistic touch. Nothing could more exasperate the Crusaders against the Saracens than thus to represent the latter as having received, and afterwards renounced, the faith.

The mention of the instruments of the Passion brings forward the Holy Lance, and especial attention must have been called to it by the extraordinary fraud which gave out that the Lance had been found at the siege of Antioch in 1098; see Gibbon's Decline and Fall, ch. lviii. Hence it is introduced naturally enough at the appearance of the Graal, as mentioned in Malory's Morte Darthur, bk. xvii, ch. xx. That a bleeding lance is mentioned in Welsh traditions seems to me more a coincidence than anything else. As for the sword of David, it was invented to match the lance and shield. The "tree which Abel was slain under" (Malory's Morte Darthur, bk. xvii. ch. vi) is connected with the curious "Legend of the Cross" discussed in S. Baring Gould's "Curious Myths," 2nd Series. So also is the idea of the three trees growing into one, and the building of Solomon's ship.

Some particulars about Joseph occur in the legend of St Veronica. Accordingly, the story of Veronica is made part of the legend of Joseph. See the French versions.

I have very little doubt that the mysterious Grail-Ark, in which so many wonders were seen, as described in ll. 258—298 of the alliterative poem, was suggested by the Holy Sepulchre. This is made probable by a passage in the Anglo-Saxon version of the legend of St Veronica, edited by Goodwin for the Cambridge Antiquarian Society in 1851, p. 40. There Joseph says of himself—"ic wæs an þæra manna þe his byrgene heold, and ic myn heafod ahylde and hyne geseon wolde, ac ic þær nan þyng of hym ne geseah. Ac ic þær twegen englas geseah, ænne at þam heafdon and oðerne at þam fotum," &c.; i. e. I was one of the men who guarded his sepulchre, and bent my head and thought to see him, but I beheld there nothing of him; but I saw two angels, one at the head and the other at the foot, &c. The two angels have become sixteen.

The Holy Graal was, at first, represented as the Dish which held the Paschal Lamb on Holy Thursday. Hence its connection with the

Bread which represented Christ's body, and its supposed *sustaining* power. On Joseph's first journey from Jerusalem, it supplies the wants of his company as the manna sustained the Israelites in the wilderness. The change which resulted in connecting it more immediately with the Chalice was intended to involve it in a higher mystery.

The Grail sometimes appeared, borne by an angel, to the devout and holy. This reminds me in some degree of the old drawings in which a Cup and an Angel are introduced into that most sacred scene, only to be contemplated with humble reverence, the scene of the Agony in the Garden.

The wonders and miracles in the old Romances are due in a great measure to the requirements of the *audience;* they were intended for brains half turned by the religious excitement of the Crusades. I think we shall best appreciate them, not by looking in them for any final purpose, but by simply observing how easily the writers drift from one idea to another. Tennyson's Holy Grail is a different conception altogether, from a higher point of view. Very much more after their manner are such poems as the "Calidore" of Keats, and the passages in the Faerie Queene where the allegory is lost sight of. They had in view a general idea of idealizing Christianity, or rather religious enthusiasm, by adding to it various mysteries and religious vows ; but beyond this, the only principle which they observed was that of giving full scope to the imagination. Their motto might well have been one like that of Keats—

"Ever let the Fancy roam,
Pleasure never is at home ;
At a touch sweet Pleasure melteth,
Like to bubbles when rain pelteth ;
Then let wingèd Fancy wander
Through the thought still spread beyond her :
Open wide the mind's cage-door,
She'll dart forth, and cloudward soar.
O sweet Fancy, let her loose ! "

Postscript.—I have assumed the copy of the Alliterative Poem
in the Vernon MS. to be unique. It may here be noted that in
MS. 8252 belonging to Sir Thomas Phillipps, there is a fragment of
2 leaves, said to be in prose, entitled "Joseph," of which the first
two words are—"After tyme." I at one time thought it possible
that this might be some part of the poem here printed, but, by the
kindness of Miss Toulmin Smith, have ascertained that the subject
of it is "a fragment of the Story of the Flight into Egypt, giving an
account of the origin and virtues of the rose of Jericho—which
sprang up wherever Mary rested on her journey—and of the growth,
virtues, and gathering of 'Bawme,' which comes from bushes that
grow in the garden in Egypt where she dwelt seven years."

I take the opportunity of mentioning here a recently published
book, by Dr Gustav Oppert, on the myths of the Graal and Prester
John. It is entitled "Der Presbyter Johannes in Sage und
Geschichte;" second edition, Berlin, 1870; London, Trübner and
Co. The same author has written an interesting paper having reference to Prester John, read Jan. 11, 1870, and printed in the Journal
of the Ethnological Society of London.

As to the "rode of northdore of london," mentioned at p. 44,
l. 217, I find that Pecock mentions it as a favourite object of pilgrimage :—"wherfore it is vein, waast, and idil forto trotte to
Wa[l]singam rather than to ech other place in which an ymage of
Marie is, and to the *rode of the north dore at London* rather than to
ech other roode in what euer place he be."—Pecock's Repressor, ed.
C. Babington, i. 194.

I observe in a book-catalogue the following entry :—

"Sainct Greaal. Cest lhystoire du sainct Greeal Qui est le
premier liure de la Table ronde. Lequel tmicte de plusieurs matieres
recreatiues. Ensemble la queste dudict sainct Greaal. Faicte par
Lancelot, Galaad, Boors, et Perceual. Qui est le dernier liure de la
table ronde, 2 vols. in 1, *woodcuts*, **Black letter**, *very fine copy in
morocco extra, gilt edges by Duru*, £100. *Paris, Phelippa Le Noir*,
1523.

One of the rarest and most sought of the Prose Romances of
Chivalry, pronounced by Dunlop the scarcest of those relating to the
Knights of the Round Table."

[Joseph of Aramathie.]

[*Vernon MS. fol.* 403.]

. . . . sire," he seis · " and soneꝛday is nouwe."

¶ þenne alle lauhwhen an heiȝ · þat herden his wordes,

" Hit is two and fourti winter," þei seiȝen · " trewely
forsoþe,

Siþen þou souȝtest þis put · and to prison eodest !"   4

" It is now
Sunday," said
Joseph.

" You have been
in prison 42
years," they said.

" Now I þonke my lord," seide Ioseph · " þat lente
me of his grace ;

me þinkeþ but þreo niȝt · al þis ilke þrowe."

¶ þenne Ioseph askes fontston · & is I-folwed blyue ;

þei solewen him and his wyf · & with him ful monye.   8

¶ Siþen com vàspasians · and was furst sped,

In þe nome of þe fader · Ioseph him folewede,

And hedde I-turned to þe seyþ · fifti with him-seluen.

¶ Siþen he sette his fader with a ferde · and a-ȝeyn
fondet,   12

þer þei bosked hem out · þat hudden hem in huirenes,

Made hem to huppe · half an hundret foote,

forte seche boþem · þer þei non seiȝen.

¶ þus þei ladden þe lyf · and lengede longe,   16

þat luyte liked his leyk · þer as he lengede.

¶ Feole flowen for fert · out of heore cuþþe

in-to Augrippus lond · was heroudes eir,

þere monye lenginde weore · for-let of heore oune.   20

" It seemed but 3
nights ! "

Joseph baptizes
Vespasian.

Vespasian and his
father make the
Jews who had hid
themselves leap
down into the
pit.

Many flee for fear
to the land of
Agrippa.

þEn com a vois to Ioseph · and seide him þise wordes,
   Biddes him and his wyf · and his sone eke,
And alle þat þey mouȝten gete · and to god tornen,
¶ Gon out of Ierusalem · & prechen hise wordes,   24
And neuer more come a-ȝeyn · whon þei weore enes þenne.

¶ In þe morwe he was sone boun · don as he biddes ;
Ioseph and his cumpanye · keueren on swiþe.
¶ Ioseph ferde bi-foren · and þe flote folewede ;   28
in-to þe lond of betanye · þis buirnes nou wenden.

¶ þei carke for here herbarwe · summe be-hynde ;
whon Ioseph herde þer-of · he bad hem not demayȝen :
" He þat ledes vs þis wei · vre herborwe schal wisse." 32
þei founden hit newely · so wel weore þei neuere.

¶ A-morwe þei weore diȝt · and don hem to ȝonge,
And come to a Forest · with floures ful feire,
þat was called Argos · þat þe kyng ouȝte,   36
in þe lond of damas · þe cuntre was dere.

þEnne spekes a vois to Ioseph · was Ihesu crist him-selue,
" Iosep[h], marke on þe treo · and make a luytel whucche,
Forte do in þat ilke blod · þou berest a-boute ;   40
¶ whon þe lust speke with me · lift þe lide sone,
þou schalt fynde me redi · riȝt bi þi syde,
And, bote þou and þi sone · me no mon touche.
And Iosep[h], walk in þe world · & preche myne wordes   44
to þe proudest men · A parti schul þei here.
¶ þauȝ þei þe of manas · melen, and þe þreten,
beo þou no þing a-dred · for non schal þe derue."
¶ " lord, I was neuer clerk · what and I ne cunne ?" 48
" Louse þi lippes a-twynne · & let þe gost worche ;
Speche, grace, & vois · schul springe of þi tonge,
& alle turne to þi mouþ · holliche atenes."

Side notes:
Joseph is bidden to go away from Jerusalem.
Next day they all start.
Some are anxious, but Joseph comforts them.
They come to the forest of Argos, in Damascus.
Christ bids Joseph to make a little box for the blood,
and to preach the gospel,
trusting to the power of the Holy Ghost.

¶ þenne he wawes his fot · þe blod he wiþ him fonges, 52
and in þe nome of þe fader · forþward he weendes.

Þei ferden to A Cite · faste bi-syde,
  þat was called sarras · þer sarsyns sprongen,
Erest þorw Abrahames wyf · þat wonede þer-inne.   56
Ioseph teiȝ to non hous · bote euene to þe temple :
He seiȝ þe kyng þer he sat · and wuste þat he was
  wraþþed,
& hopede he scholde him · touward God turne ;
For he and þo of Egipte ·han werret to-gedere,   60
And þei discounfitede him han · and scaþet ful ofte.
¶ þe kyng and his Baronage · a counseil bi-gonnen ;
he wolde haue red of his folk · and fare to hem ȝitte ;
& þei forsaken hit han · & he vnsauht sittes.   64

" Sire," seis Iosep[h] · " or semblaunt is feble,
  In gret Anguisse ȝe ben · þat nis not God greiþe ;
wolde ȝe herkene to me · icholde ow bi-heete,
He þat is mi foundeor · may hit folfulle,   68
þat was ded on þe cros · & bouȝte us so deore ;
I am not worþi to seyn · moni of his werkes."
¶ " þou schewest A symple skil," quaþ þe kyng · " of-
  scutered þou semest
to speke of A ded mon · what may he don þer-ate ?" 72
¶ "I schal sei ou," quod Ioseph · "& ȝe wol vndurstonde."
" tel ou," seis þe kyng · " þi tale wol I here."

" Þat tyme þat Augustus Cesar · was Emperour of
    Rome,
þis reson bi-gon · þat I schal now rikenen,   76
¶ whon god·sende an Angel · in-to Galile,
to A Cite, bi nome · Nazareth I-called,
to A Maiden ful meke · þat Marie was hoten,
And seide, ' Blessed beo þou flour · feirest of alle ! 80
þe holigost wiþ-Inne þe · schal lenden and lihte ;
þou schalt beren a Child · schal Ihesu bi hoten.'

They come to Sarras.

Joseph hopes to convert the king.

The king holds a council.

Joseph promises to help the king, conditionally.

The king wonders how Christ can still have power,

and bids Joseph explain.

"God sent an angel to Nazareth,

to tell Mary that she should bear a son.

he chau*n*gede cher & seide · 'hou scholde I gon wit*h*
   childe
wit*h*-oute felauschupe of mon?' · he bad hire not
   demayen ;   84
¶ ' þou schalt be mayden for hi*m* · bi-foreñ, and after.
Holliche wit*h*-oute*n* wem · wite þou forsoþe.'
And heo grau*n*tede þenne · to ben at his grace ;
And sone aftur þat gretnede · þat greiþli Mayde.   88

W hon he wolde ben I-bore*n* · at a Blisful tyme,
   he dude Miracles feole · þat mony men seiȝen ;
þre kynges of þe Est · þroly þei comen,
And vche put hi*m* in hond · [a] *present* ful riche.   92
¶ Soone Heroudes þe kyng · herde of his burþe ;

He lette sle for his sake · selli mony childre*n* ;
Foure þousend and seue score · was þe su*m*me holden,
þat weore I-slawe for his sake · for certeyn hit telles ; 96
Bote þorwȝ þe grace of hi*m*-self · gete hi*m* heo ne miȝt.

His Mooder ay wit*h* hi*m* fleih · forþ in-to Egipte.
¶ Whon he com in-to þe lond · leeue þou forsoþe,
feole te*m*ples þer-inne · tulten to þe eorþe,   100
for heore false ymages · þat þei on leeueden.

Do a-wei þi Maumetes · þei han trayed þe ofte ;
Let breken he*m* a-two · and bren hem al to pouder,
Schaltou neue*r* gete grace · þorwȝ none suche goddes."

¶ þenne seis þe kyng · "my wit mai not leeue,   105
þat þou ne melest wonderli · & most a-ȝeyn kuynde.
Hou scholde a child come forþ · wit*h*-oute flescly dedes
Bi-twene wo*m*mon and Mon ? · my wit may not leeue."

"S Ire," seide Ioseph · " þou hiȝtest me to heere,   109
   And I schal *p*reue þe tale · þat I fore telle.

¶ whon god sat in his blisse · bosked in heuene,
He seiȝ þe peple þorw peine · passen in-to helle.   112
also wel þe holyeste · heold þider euene
as þe moste fooles ; · and þe fader þouȝte

þat hit seemede nouȝt · and wolde his sone sende
forte briuge hem out þer-of · and þerfore he lihte "— 116

and sent forth His Son."

" **W**hat, mou ? " quaþ þe kyng · " þou castest þi-
      seluen.
Toldest þou not now bi-foren · he nedde neuer fader,
but elles, wiþ-oute mon · I-bore of a Mayden ?
And þou seist now he has on · hou may þis sitte same ? "
¶ " He was Fader," quod Ioseph · "and for his sake called,
þat was gostliche his halt · ar he weore mon formed ;
And of two persones · sprong out þe þridde ;
þat was þe holigost · as I be-foren seide. 124
His godhede lees he nouȝt · þeiȝ he come lowe,
þat he nas god ay forþ · in his grete strengþe.
¶ I sei þe Fader was God · ar out was bi-gonnen,
Made alle þing of nouȝt · þorw miht of him one, 128
Dude þe prophetes to seye · þat hem-self nuste,
Bote as hit com heom to mouþ · and meleden þe wordes.
þe kuynde of þe Moder · þat he on eorþe tok,
þat diȝede a-wei · for he hit most dredde. 132
Bote þe kuynde of his Fader · þat was þe furste kuynde,
Holliche euere he heold · for þat diȝede neuere.
Bote he was gostliche of Fader · and fleschliche of Moder,
So þat he com twies forþ · and bi two kuyndes." 136

"Now you say Jesus had a Father," says the king.

"He was His ghostly Father.

The Father is God the Creator.

Jesus never lost His Father's nature, being twice born."

ÞEnne seis þe kyng · " þe lengore I here,
     þe lesse reson I seo · in þat þat þou rikenest.
¶ þou toldest furst of his Fader · and of his furste
     kuynde,
And þreo persones · and alle þei ben goddes." 140
¶ " ȝe, sire, bote I pertly vndo · þat I haue þe profred,
I am worþi muche blame · what mai I seiȝe more ?
¶ þe sone, I tolde bi-fore · fongede vr kuynde,
tok flesch and blod · in a feir mayden ; 144
his Godhede luttulde not · þeiȝ he lowe lihte,
þat he nas euere of o miȝt · mensked he worþe ! "

The king is still more confused.

"The Son took on Him man's nature, but lost not His Godhead."

  ¶ þe kyng fette forþ · feole of his clerkes,

  to spute wiþ Ioseph · þat spedes hem luite. 148

Joseph defeats all who dispute with him.

  Ioseph tok þe holy writ · and tei for his teeme,

  and destruyede heore tale · wiþ-inne þreo wordes.

  ¶ þe ky[n]g bi-heold on his face · and on his limes lowore,

  Say; he was barefot · and bar him in herte, 152

The king admires Joseph,

  He[1] hedde I-ben of hei; blod · hedde he ben I-bosket,

  And a ferli feir mon · and witerli him rewes.

and asks his name. "Joseph of Aramathie."

  ¶ "what hettestou," seis þe kyng · to Iosep[h] þenne.

  "Ioseph of Aramathie · is mi nome called." 156

  "I schal sei þe, Ioseph · as my wit þinkes,

  þow semest not ful good clerk · to kenne suche wordes ;

  þe tale is hei; in him-self · þat þou of tellest,

"Thy tale is dark ; come again to-morrow."

  Hit is ful þester to me · & moni a mon eke. 160

  ¶ I schal seie þe, Ioseph · I haue to done swiþe ;

  I may not wel lenge now · to-morwe meet me heere ;

  þow schalt haue liueraunce of In · and al þat þe neodes ;

  whon vre leyser is more · vre lustnynge is bettre." 164

"I have 50 companions."

  ¶ "I haue felauschupe wiþ-outen," seis Iosþph · "wel a-boute fifti,

  Boþe wymmen and men · þat mote wiþ me Inne."

The king sends for them all, and inquires about Joseph's son, named Josaphe.

  ¶ þe kyng lette fette hem forþ · bi-foren him to seo,

  what leodes þei beon · and where þei weore boren ;— 168

  "I trouwe þat beo þi sone " · bi Iosaphe he seide.

  ¶ ";e, sire, so he is · for soþe as I þe telle."

  "Con he out of clergye ?" · seis þe kyng þenne.

  "leeue me forsoþe, sire · þer liues no bettre." 172

All are well lodged.

  ¶ þe kyng lette lede hem · in-to toun lowe,

  to a feir old court · and Innes hem þere.

The king at night had three cares,

N ow we leuen Ioseph · and of þe kyng carpen ;

  As he lai at niht · keuered in bedde, 176

  In þreo þou;tes he was · and þat weore þis ilke :

  ¶ On for his grete folk · þat him wiþ-sakon hedde ;

         ¹ MS. "He he hedde."

¶ A-noþur for Iosep[h]s tale · þat wolde sayn he tornede;

¶ þe þridde, How God scholde wiþ-outen wem · wonen

   in a Mayden.   180

the *third* being
how God could
dwell in a maiden.

¶ Þenne he seih in his chaumbre-flor · þreo[1] souht vp

   at ones.

All at once he
sees three trees,
with equal stems,

þe braunches on heiȝ weoren · alle of o lengþe ;

Bote þe bark of þat on · semede dimmore

but one had a
darker bark.

þen ouþer of þe oþer two · trouwe þou forsoþe ;   184

¶ þat signede Ihesu crist · for sake[2] of vre kuynde,

was nout out-wiþ so cler · bote wiþ-inne he was clene.

¶ He calles on his chaumberleyn · to kennen vncouþes,

He calls his
chamberlain.

And he rises a-non · and for ferd falles.   188

And he feres[3] him vp · and bad him not ben ferd ;

" þer schal falle non euel · of þat is here formed."

¶ þei lihten two torches · and to þis trees wenten ;.

They examine the
trees.

þei weore semeli bi-neoþe · þei mihte not seo þe heiȝþe,

sprongen wiþ gret sped · of a good spice.   193

On vche braunche was a word · of þreo maner enkes ;

Each stem bore a
word, in three
inks, gold, silver,
and blue.

Gold and Seluer he seis · and Asur forsoþe.

¶ "'þis makeþ,'" quod þe wiht · "þe marke of gold ; "

¶ "And 'þis saues,'" quaþ þat wiht · "þe seyne of seluer;

And 'þis clanses' · as þe Asur kennes."

[Fol. 463 b, col. 1.]

¶ þe kyng nuste wel forte seye · bi wit þat he hedde,

The king cannot
tell if he sees one
or three trees.

wheþer þat he seȝe · was on forte sigge,   200

oþer two, or þreo · or what he miȝte telle.

¶ þe kyng was a-bascht · and to his bed buskes ;

and his Chaumberleyn so a-ferd · þat neih he felde I-

   swowen.

¶ þenne he seiȝ a newe chaumbre-wouh · wrouȝt al of

   bordes,   204

Next he sees a
partition of
boards, with a
child coming
through a door
in it.

a dore honginge þer-on · haspet ful faste,

---

[1] May we read " þreo *treos*," inserting *treos* on the strength
of l. 191 ? The passage seems partly corrupt.

[2] MS. " forsake."

[3] So in MS. Perhaps we should read " beres." See the
Glossarial Index.

8

A child cominge þorw · his come was nout seene,
Siþen lenges a while · and a-ʒein lendes,
wiþ-outen faute oþer faus · as þei fore seiden.   208
¶ þenne spekes a vois · and on heiʒ sigges,
"king, haue þou no ferli · of þat is heere formed,
for so god with-outen wem · wende in a Mayden."

Now we leuen þe kyng · and of Ioseph carpen ; 212
"A ! lord !" quaþ Ioseph · "how may þis limpe
Of þis king Eualak · þat con not vnderstonde ?
Bote ʒif I turne him bi þis poynt · ar he henne passe,
beos he neuermore I-tornd · treweli I trouwe.   216
Nou I be-seche þe, Ihesu · as þou art ful of Ioye,
þat speke to hem of Israel · þorw Moyses speche,
And bad þei schulde leeuen · for no-skunus þinge,
In non oþur straunge god · bote studefast þe holde : 220
And wustest daniel in þe put · þat he was inne I-worpe
Among þe leones feole · þat he no scaþe lauʒte :
And for-ʒaf þe Maudeleyn · mekelyche hire sunnes :
And siþen seidest to me · mi preyere scholde sitte ; 224
þou heiʒtest holichurche · to haunsen hire strengþe,
to hiʒen þi godhed · hit helpes nout elles ;
Nou, gloriouse kyng · graunte me mi boone."

þenne spekes a vois · and on heiʒ sigges,   228
"Ioseph, haue þou no care · þe kyng schal sone
torne :
Go þou most to þi wyf · gete þou most nede
A child, Galaad schal be hoten · þat goodnesse schal
reise
þe Auenturus of Brutayne · to haunsen and to holden."
And he dos as he bad · and to his bed buskes.   233
¶ In þe morwe he was vppe · and roises þis oþure.
þenne hit þester bi-gon · and þonderde swiþe,
þat þe graue quakede · and þei a-grisen alle.   236
¶ He bi-þenkes him þo · and to his whucche weendes,

And ſeole preiers he made · þat Iheſu criſt herde,

And ſpekes to hem · wiþ loueliche wordes.

¶ " I-bleſſet be ȝe to day · alle myne leoue children "—

And he tolde hem of his crucifiing · hou he [þe] cros

    ſouȝte,   241

And of heore fadres bi-fore · þat he ſond vn-kuynde—

" Er þei ſpeeken to me ſeire · and ſaynede me wiþ

    wordes,

Bote þei hateden me · and hedden de-deyn.   244

Bote beo ȝe ſtable in oure fei · and foleweþ vre werkes,

for ȝe han more of þe lawe · þen prophetes hedden.

¶ þei nedden bote þe holygoſt · and ſo ȝe han eke,

and ſiþen bodiliche me · to ben at or wille.   248

¶ I nul not faſtenen on þe ſone · þe Fadres gultus,

I for-ȝiue ow clene · þe harm þat I hedde.

And cum þou hider, Ioſaphe · for þou art Iugget clene,

And art digne þer-to · þat dos me to lyke;   252

Ichul bi-take þe to-day · in a good tyme

on þe hiȝeſte þing · holden on eorþe,

non oþer of me · hit murili to habben,

but elles vche mon of þe · þat takes hit aftur."   256

He bad him lifte vp · and þe lide warpes :—

þenne he ſeos Iheſu criſt · in a ſad Roode,

    and his fyue Angeles · þat forþ wiþ him ſtoden,

As red as þe fuir · and he hem bi-holdes.   260

¶ þat on beres in his hond · a cros of queynte hewe ;

¶ þat oþer beres in his hond · þreo blodi nayles ;

¶ þe þridde þe Coroune · þat his hed keuerde ;

¶ þe Feorþe, þe launce · þat lemede him wiþ-Inne ;   264

¶ And þe Fyfþe a blodi cloþ · þat he was inne i-braced,

whon he lay after ſlauht · in þe ſepulcre.

¶ þenne he falles for fere · forþ wiþ þe wȝucche ;

Eft he bad him riſe vp · he ros wiþ þe bone.   268

¶ þenne he ſauh Iheſu criſt · I-ſtrauȝt vppon þe Roode,

whuche þe Angel by-fore · hedde in his hond ;

Christ speaks to Joseph,

bidding him to be steadfast in the faith.

"Josaphe, thou art worthy ; I will confer on thee a very great gift."

Josaphe sees Christ on the cross, and five angels, bearing

(1) the cross, (2) the nails, (3) the crown of thorns, (4) the lance, and (5) a cloth.

Next he sees Christ stretched out upon the cross,

And þe þreo nayles · þat þe oþur bi-foren hedde,
In his honden and his feet · alle þei weore faste ;   272

¶ Siþen stiken wiþ þe spere · blod and watur louses ;
Bi-holdes touward hise feet · say fro hem renne ;
eornen al of red blod · romynge a-boute ;
Al priueliche his peyne · a-pertliche he sauh.   276

"WHi lengest þou," quod Iosep[h] · to his sone,
          "so longe ?
And so stille liggest · lokynde in þe whucche ? "

"A ! Fader, touche me not · in þis ilke tyme,
For muche gostliche grace · me is here I-graunted."   280
¶ þenne þei loken in atte wзucche · loueliche boþe,
¶ þenne þei seзen Ihesu crist · in þat ilke foorme,
þat heo seзen him sodeynliche · whon heo furst comen
aftur þe slauзt to him · to þe sepulcre.   284

¶ þenne comen two Angeles · wiþ twayles white,
And eiþer bar in his hond · a basyn of seluer ;
Oþur Tweyne aftur hem · with cruetes sone,
and wasscheles wiþ haly water · with hem þei brouзten ;

And oþer two after hem · with sencers *soone,   289
set wiþ riche stones · and a viole of sence.

¶ þen com on, 'þe strengþe of god' · gabriel I-hoten,
wiþ þe riccheste sege · þat euer for secte seemes ;   292

And oþer two after him · wiþ crois and wiþ Mitre,
And oþure bouwynde after · wiþ vestimens sone.

HE seiз an Auter I-cloþed · wiþ cloþes ful riche ;
    Vppon þat on ende lay · þe launce and þe nayles,
And vppon þat oþer ende · þe disch wiþ þe blode,   297
and a vessel of gold · geynliche bi-twene.

¶ Ihesu made for to greiþe Iosaphe · in þat geyn weede,
And sacrede him to Bisschop · wiþ boto his hondes,   300
And tolde him of his vestimens · what þei signefyen ;
In vche Cite þere he come · sacren on he scholde
wiþ þe selue oygnemens · þat he to him wrouзte.

And an-oyg[n]ten oþer kynges · þat to crist torneden. 304

¶ ȝit he leres him more · loueliche him-seluen—

" I beo-take þe her, Iosaphe · soules to kepe ;

ȝif eni þorw þi defaute · falle fro my riche,

At þe day of Iuggement · þou beost ioyned harde ; 308

¶ I seiȝe, Ioseph þi fader · schal bodiliche hem ȝeme,

And þou gostliche · nou ȝemes hem boþe.

wiþ-drawe þe of þi vestimens · and do hem vp to holde ;

Go now to-ward þe court · þe kyng for to turne." 312

Þ Enne þei wenden heore wei · and to þe court ȝongen,

And al a-boute þe paleys · haly water þei spreynden,

for mony a wikkede gost · woned hedde þere.

¶ wiþ-outen, on þe paleys · as þei bi passeden, 316

werdes of Ebreu · weren I-writen of ȝore,

And sein, ' daniel of Babiloyne · whon he fro Batayle wente

Fro nabugodonosor · þe kyng þat him hade,

called þis paleis " Auntres " · and forsoþe seide, 320

þat hit scholde trewely · in sum tyme aftur,

called beo þe paleis · merueilouse for werkes,

þat þer scholde beo seyȝen · þorw sonde of vr lord.'

¶ Bi þat was A Messager come · after þis men sone ; 324

whon þei comen to þe halle · þei maden þe signe

on hem of þe verrey cros · and toward þe kyng eoden.

¶ þe kyng hedde geten him a clerk · on of þe beste,

nouȝwhere in heore lawe · was such a-nother holden, 328

to take Ioseph in his tale · ȝif he wrong seide.

¶ " þou toldest me ȝusterday," quod þe kyng · " þou wost wel þi-seluen,

Of þise þreo persones · and alle þei beoþ goddes ;

And siþen of a-noþer · wonder forsoþe, 332

þat Ihesu with-outen wem · won in a Mayden."

" Þ at I tolde þe þo · I telle þe ȝitte ;

I nul forsake my word · for no maner þinge."

The clerk
disputes, and
denies the
Trinity.

Op stondes þis clerk · and seis him þise wordes,   336
" Ʒif þise þreo persones · þat þou þe fore puttest
han bote on godhede · þei nare not goddes alle ;
Ʒif vchon haue a godhede · I graunte, bi him-selue,
I seie þat on is also good · as þe þreo hole.   340
¶ þat on is a verrei god · I sei bi god greyþe ;
þis oþer two nare none · in no maner þinge."
He sprong in his sputison · and speek harde wordes,
þat Ioseph hedde no space · while his speche laste. 344

Josaphe reminds
the king of last
night's dream,

¶ Op stondes Iosaphe · and þe fader sittes,
Speek wiþ an heiʒ vois · þat al þe folk herde,
" Nou þe greteþ, sir Euelak · God of israel
þorw his seruauntes mouþ · and seye þe I wile.   348
¶ þou hast I-seʒe to-niht · signefies summe,
þow hast diskeueret hem · þer he nis not payet,
Heere þou schalt ha vengaunce · verreyliche and sone,
þat al þi reume schal seo · þat þou wrong siggest ; 352

and says that
Tholomer, king
of Babylon,
will take the king
and kill him.

¶ For he, þis ilke Tholomer · þat þou weore wont to
     hunte,
þat is kyng of Babiloyne · hiderward he buskes ;
þreo dayes with þe niht · nou he þe schal driue,
Siþen lacche þe atte laste · and þe þi lyf bi-reuen ; 356
He þat dorste nere ʒut · þe nouʒwhere a-byde,
nou schal winne his wille of þe · for þi wrong bi-leeue."

The clerk again
gets up to speak,
but his eyes fly
out of his head.

¶ þenne stod vp þis clerk · and wolde eft dispuite ;
þenne him þouʒte þat on · heold him bi þe tonge,   360
And he roungede an heiʒ · and rorede so harde,
his eiʒen flowen out of his hed · and biforen him fallen.

¶ þenne vp sturten þe folk · and wolden wiþ wepene
     sle Iosep[h] and his sone · for sake[1] of þis
     oþer ;   364

King Evelak
protects Joseph,

And þe kyng Eualac · cauʒte his swerd sone,
And beo þe miht of Iubiter · he swor to hem alle,

[1] MS. "forsake," as in l. 185.

weore eny of heom so wood · heom forte founde,
he wolde felle hem seye · ar þei þenne ferden.   368
¶ þenne seis þe kyng · " mai þer out me helpe
forto saue me out · ȝif þat hit so lym[p]e ? "
¶ " ȝe, sire," seis Iosaphe · " to fonge þe trouþe."
" And what trouwest þou of þis mon · tides him hele ? "
" Gos to oure Maumetes · and proues heore mihtes."
¶ þenne þei taken þis mon · and towen him to þe
    temple,
A-non þei brouȝten him forþ · bi-foren þe moste mayster,
Calleþ vppon an ymage · þat Appolliñ hette,   376
and wol not onswere a word · þauh þei scholde swelten.
¶ þenne spekes an ymage · in a-noþer huirne,
þat ȝe clepeþ Martis · " nouȝt is þat ȝe mene ;
Appolin is bounden · and braset so faste,   380
he may not speke a word · for no þing alyue."

þenne Ioseph hente a staf · þat stod him bi-syde,
    strikes to þis Appolin · with a strong wille,
þat his nekke to-barst · and brak al to pouder,   384
and þe fend of his bodi · fleyȝ to þe lufte.
¶ þenne þei leuen him þer · and goþ *touward oþure ;
¶ þe kyng bowes to his pors · him offring to beode.
" Let beo," seis Iosaphe · " I leeue þe beo bettre ;   388
For and þou profre him eny · I schal do [þe] to preue,
vppon sodeyne deþ · þou schalt sone dye."
¶ " Do tel me," seis þe kyng · " I haue þe muche truste,
Of þis tholomer and me · hou schal hit tyden ? "   392
And he onsweres aȝeyn · " I dar not wel sigge,
for þis cristene men · þat vmbe mong ȝongen.
¶ Se ȝe not þe tweyne Angeles · leden hem a-boute ?
¶ þat on bereþ a cros · þat oþer a swerd kene ;   396
¶ wher-so-euere þei ben stad · such is heore strengþe,
Vre maystrie is nouȝt · in no maner þinge."
¶ þenne seis Iosaphe · " for us ne schalt þou wonde ;
Vppon þe heiȝe trinite · I halse þe to telle,   400

and asks if there
is any help, and
if the blind clerk
will recover.

Josaphe bids him
go and ask the
idols.

Appollin will
give no answer.

Mars says
Appollin is
bound fast.

Joseph breaks
Appollin in
pieces.

[* Fol. 404, col. 1.]

The king
questions another
idol,

who says he sees
two angels with
Joseph.

Josaphe conjures
the idol to tell
all ;

Spek al þat þou const · & let þe kyng here."

"Of newe þing þat is to come," he seis · "con I not
telle."

Bi þat was a Messager i-come · and to þe kyng menes,
And seis him þat tholomer · has taken of his londes.

¶ "þe riche Cite of Nagister · nomen he has forsoþe ;
Siþen he keueres vppon · and takes bi-fore clene   406
þe Castel of a-longines · and hiderward he ioynes,
with sixti þousent," he seide · "of clene men of Armes,
And Fifti þousend fot-men · þat redi beþ to fihte,   409
þei han geten þat holt · for certeyn soþe ;
þer is non in þat lond · þat schal hem wiþstonden."
¶ þenne þe kyng was a-ferd · I hete þe forsoþe,   412
leste þe tale of Iosaphe · ferede trewe.

ÞE kyng boskes lettres a-non · to bounen his bernes,
Comaundes hem to meeten him · tymely on þe
morwen,
At þe Castel of Carboye · þer he beden hade,   416
was fiftene myle · fro sarras I-holden,
And oþer fiftene myle · fro þenne as þei leiȝen.
¶ þenne Ioseph takes him forþ · and seiþ him þis
wordes,
"wostou what þou do, kyng · nou þat þou wendes ?
Of þi comynge a-ȝein · const þou not telle.   421
¶ Such signe me is tauȝt · þou art of cun symple ;
forsoþe A mon was þi fader · þat couþe schon a-mende !
¶ þat tyme þat Augustes cesar · was Emperour of Rome,
þou wast lenged in þe lond · þat þat lord ouȝte.   425
Fourti knihtes douȝtres · he wolde haue of fraunce,
forte souwe selk-werk · and sitten in his chaumbre.
¶ For þou were a feir child · þou weore I-fet to serue
twei feire maydenes · and wiþ þis mon lengedest.   429
¶ þei heolden þe of herre blod · þen þou boren weore ;
So þou souȝtes fro him · to þe erl of Surye.
So þou and his sone · vppon a day seten,   432

And ȝe woxen vn-sauȝt · and þou slouȝ him þere.

So þou come to þe kyng · þat þis kuþþe auȝte ;

Seidest þou were a kniht · and in his court laftest.

¶ He was an old mon · weried of werre,   436

And þou weore a ȝong mon · in þi grete strengþe.

For þou toke his enemy · and brouȝtest him to honde,

forþi he ȝaf þe þis lond · after his lyue.

Hit is not allynge to carpe, sire kyng · wher-of we

    comen."   440

He takes non [hede] heere-to · bote askes him of þe

    sweuene

þat he mette on þe niht · and bad he scholde him telle.

¶ "whon þat þou comest aȝeyn · wite þou schalt

    forsoþe,

þou miht haue more redi roume · my rikenyng to here !"

¶ Joseph[e] takes his scheld · and schapes a-middes

A crois of red cloþ · and kennes him aftur,   446

whon his peril weore most · to crist he scholde preyen,

for þer scholde no mon verreili · þat vigore bi-holder,

þat he nis saaf þat dai · and his sore passed.   449

Þ Enne he buskes touward þe bente · þer þis oþer
    byden,

He arayes his riche men · and rihtes hem swiþe.

A-non tholomers men · woxen þe biggore ;   452

sone beeren hem a-bac · and brouhten hem to grounde ;

And þei tornede a-ȝein · þat tyme hit was non oþer.

¶ þei come bi tholomers tentes · vn-housed hem sone,

Token holliche his stor · and a-wei streiȝten,   456

þat þei come to a Castel · faste be-syde.

¶ þe kyng was gon to pleye him · bi a water brimme,

þen com on prikynge · prest him a-ȝeynes.

He seide, "my ladi þe queene · ou a lettre sende,   460

Biddes ou wihtly be boun · to don as heo biddes."

And he redes hit forþ · and fond þer-on sone,

þat he scholde wiþ-drawe him · al a-wei þenne,

Thou didst slay the earl of Syria's son,

and didst come to the court of the old king of Sarras."

The king asks about his dream.

Josaphe makes a cross of red cloth on Evelak's shield.

Evelak arrays his men.

Tholomer's men get the best of it,

but their enemies spoil their tents.

Evelak receives a letter from his queen,

bidding him to retreat.

Or elles tholomers folk · wol take*n* him þere ;   464

¶ Forþi heo wolc þat he wite · and warnes hi*m* beo-
time.

¶ "Ho has witered hire of þis · and ho has hire
ke*n*ned ? "

He onsweres a-non · " sire, I not forsoþe.

Evelak learns
that Joseph and
his son have
warned the
queen.

Bote þe two cristene men · þat bydes ow at court,   468
in gret cou*n*seil han I-beo · I trouwe hit be þer a-
boute ; "—

And he telles hem þenne · of þe qwene sonde
þorw cou*n*seil of Iosaphe · and Ih*e*su þei þonken.

The king collects
14,000 more men.

¶ Þ E kyng Boskes lettres a-non · to boune mo bernes ;
    bi þat þe niȝt was a-weye · And þe day on þe
    morwe,   473
þei hadde*n* of newe folk · fourtene þousend.

He sees 500 men
approaching,

He seiȝ vnder a wode-egge · siker bi hem-seluen
Freschliche I-diht · Fyue hondred men of Armes.   476
¶ On vn-castes his helm · and to þe kyng rydes,

their captain
being Seraphe,
his wife's brother.

And he kneuȝ him wel · he was his wynes broþer,
was I-called Seraphe · a ȝong Erl forsoþe,
and a douȝti þer-wiþ · in alle goode deedes ;   480

[* Fol. 404, col. 2.]

He mihte neuer gete loue of þe kyng · much * ne luyte,
ne good herte of him · and he non harm seruede.

Seraphe says the
queen has sent
him.

He seide, " my ladi þe Qwene · me a lettre sende,   483
Ȝif euere I halp hire at neode · I scholde hit now cuiþe ;
And I am come to þi wille · sire, wiþ þis knihtes."
" Forsoþe," he seis, " seraphe · so þou euele ouȝtest ;
Ofte I haue for-set þe · þat me sore forþinkes,
For euere þe kuynde wol be frend · for ouȝt þat mai
bi-falle."   488

They go to meet
the enemy.

N ow þei bouwe touward þe bente · þe*r* þis oþere
    houen ;
He arayes his riche men · and rihtes hem bettre,
þat þorw him reowen no res · þat his red wrouȝten.

¶ þenne seis Seraphe · "holdes ou stille, 492

And þenkes on, goode men · þe gref is oure childre ;
what wol bi-falle þer-of · and we ben confoundet.
Betere hit were douhtilyche · to diȝen on or oune,
þen wiþ schendschupe to schone · and vs a-bak drawe."
þei han geten on hem · þe lengþe of a gleyue : 497
¶ whon Seraphe seiȝ þat men · þei miȝte I-seo sone
his pollhache go · and proude doun pallede.
In þe þikkeste'pres · he preuede his wepne, 500

Breck braynes a-brod · brusede burnes,
Beer bale in his hond · bed hit a-boute.
He hedde an hache vppon heiȝ · wiþ a gret halue,
Iluld hit harde wiþ teis · in his two hondes ; 504
So he frusschede hem with · and fondede his strengþe,

þat luyte miȝte faren him fro · and to fluiȝt founden.
¶ þere weore stedes to struien · stoures to medlen,
Meeten miȝtful men · mallen þorw scheldes, 508

¶ Harde hauberkes to-borsten · and þe brest þurleden.
Schon schene vppon schaft · schalkene blode.
¶ þo þat houen vppon hors · heowen on helmes.
¶ þo þat hulden hem on fote · hakken þorw scholdres.
mony swouȝninge lay · þorw schindringe of scharpe,

And starf aftur þe deþ · in a schort while.
¶ þer weoren hedes vn-huled · helmes vphaunset ;
harde scheldes to-clouen · on quarters fellen, 516
slen hors and mon · holliche at enes.

Þ̵E stiward of Eualak · in þe stour lafte,

lai streiht on þe feld · striken to þe eorþe.
¶ Now Eualac and tholomer · twies han a-semblet ;
Seraphe takes of heore men · wel a two hundred, 521

to wende to a Roche · was faste bi-syde.
Hedde þei geten þat holt · for certeyne soþe,
þei mihten haue do muche harm · er þei han hem mihte.
¶ þenne com on wiþ a tale · and Tholomer he telles,
And seis him hou Seraphe · has his men serued ; 526

His broþer and a batayle · weore bosket bi-sydes,
And he sende him word · he scholde þider seche,

And þei come swiftly vppon · and swengeden to-gedere.

¶ Seraphe was of hem wel war · and faste hem a-scries ;

He mette a gome on an hors · with a gret route,

He hente vp his hachet · and huttes him euene,   532

Al to-hurles þe helm · and þe hed vnder.

wiþ þe deþ in his hals · dounward he duppes,

and þat deruede hem muche · on þat oþer syde,

for þe kyng Tholomer · was treweli his broþer.   536

¶ þen Seraphe fondes in · he and fourti knihtes,

¶ þer þe batayle was stiffest · and of more strengþe.

¶ þenne þei fullen for grame · to Seraphe knihtes ;

þei han laft him a-lyue · but vnneþe seuene.   540

Sikerli þe seuene · weore slayen at þe laste,

Him wondet þer-wiþ · and wemmet so sore,

þat he was in swounynge · and fel to þe grounde.

¶ Sone þenne he starte vp · and streiȝte to his hache,

culles on mennes hedes · þat þei doun lyen,   545

Siþen cacches his hors · and a-wei wendes.

Bote euer-more Seraphe · askes and cries,

" where was Eualac ? " · þe stour was so þikke.   548

¶ wel a fyue þousend men · of tholomeres halue

weore bytwene hem two · þat to him he ne mihte,

And he nedde bote fourti men · folewynde his brydel.

And þei were weri of-fouȝten · and feor ouer-charged,

Of þe peple afurst · and þe pres after ;   553

luyte wonder hit was · so þey wrouȝt haden.

Þenne was Eualac taken · and woundet ful sore ;

And þe kyng tholomer · takes him to kepe,   556

Ferde in-to a forest · faste bi-syde,

forte fallen him feye · er þei a-ȝeyn ferden.

¶ þenne he vn-keuered his scheld · & on þe cros bi-
          holdes ;

He seiȝ a child strauȝt þer-on · stremynge on blode,   560

And he bi-souȝte him of grace · as he was godes foorme.

¶ þenne he seiȝ a whit kniht · comynge him a-ȝeines, A white knight comes to his rescue,
boþe Armure and hors · al as þe lilye,
A red cros on his scheld · seemed him feire ;   564
Rydes to tholomer · rad wiþ þat ilke,
Baar him doun of his hors · and harmed him more, and slays Tholomer.
strok him stark ded · þat he sturede neuere.
¶ Siþen he fonges forþ · a ferly wepne,   568
fel hem feiȝe to his feet · þat him hedde folewed.
¶ þenne he horses Eualac · on tholomeres steede, The white knight mounts Evelak on Tholomer's horse.
houwes touward þe batayle · bigly and swiþe.
¶ Euer-more Eualac · askes and cries,   572
"where was Seraphe ?" · and seiȝ him wiþ þat ilke,
wher seue knihtes him han · sikerliche a-sayled,
and titli bi-gonnen · to take him bi þe bridel.   575
¶ þe white kniht wiþ his swerd · swyngede to hem sone ;
whon þe sixe weoren dede · þe seueþe a knyf * cauhte, [* Fol. 404 b, col. 1.] Seraphe is nearly overpowered.
And wolde ha striken Seraphe · at a stude derne,
vppon an hole of his helm · and he was so for-fouȝten
þat he hedde no space · spedly him-seluen   580
forto do him no dispit · þe sporn was his owne.
¶ whon Eualac þat sauȝ · he fel to þe grounde,
And Seraphe also · and boþe lye [a] swoune.
¶ þe white kniht lihtes doun · and boþe hem vp-liftes ; The white knight lifts up Evelak and Seraphe.
þer nas no lynde so liht · as þise two leodes,   585
whon þei blencheden a-boue · and eiþer seiȝ oþer.
¶ þenne seis Seraphe · "scheuȝ me myn hache, Seraphe asks for his axe.
and I schal note hit to-day · my strengþe is so newed."
¶ "Haue her-on," seis þe white kniht · "vppon my bi- The white knight gives him one.
halue ;   589
God sende þe þis · þat al þe grace lenes."
whon he hedde hit in honde · he heold hit þe betere,
And þe heuior bi fer · þen he bi-foren hedde ;   592
Nas þer ȝong mon ne old · þat ȝernloker wrouȝte
þen Eualac and Seraphe · wher-so-euer þei souȝten, Evelak and Seraphe are now as fresh as hawks.
Also fresch as þe hauk · freschore þat tyme,

þen þei foundeden þidere · in heore furste cume.   596
But euer-more þe white kniht · hem þe place roumede,
Hit falles not for to seiȝe · þe fere of his duntes.
þer he lousede his hond · he leyde hem on Ronkes,
and welde hem bi-foren · at his oune wille.   600

¶ þe stiward of Tholomer · stoffes hem to-gedere,
and seis, "þei ben a-middes þe Reume · and mowe not
        hom reche,
ne heo knowe not in the lond · forþi þei moten lenge."
¶ þenne þe folk of þe Roche · hem in face kepten,   604
maden þer a siker werk · and slowen hem vp clene.

Eualac and Seraphe · wonder hem þhouȝte
      wher þe white kniht bi-com · þat won hem þe
        prys ;
þei nuste where he was · ne on whuche syde.   608

¶ þenne seis Seraphe · þat hom he wolde wende,
He is woundet ful sore · to winnen his ese.
¶ "Trewely," seis Eualac · "þow schalt wiþ me to
        court,
And two wonderful men · þou schalt seo þere ;   612
þei tolde me of vche a poynt · ar I fro home wente,
al-to-gedere of þis werk · hou hit is wonne."

Nou we leuen þe kyng · and of Ioseph carpen,
      þat restes him in Sarras · bi-leued wiþ þe qweene.

"Hou trouwestou of my lord?" heo seis · "tydes him
        hele,   617
Has he folfulsened þe sawes · þat þou bi-fore seidest?"

"Ȝe, þorw þe miht of god · þe maystrie is wonnen,
And þorw his swete grace · þe sarrest is passed."   620

¶ "Ȝe, I wol bi-hote þe heer · þi lawe for to holden,
whon þat my lord is comen · þat schal I furst fongen."
"Do me sikernesse þer-to" · seis Ioseph þenne.
¶ "I wole my trouþe þe bi-take · I wol þe nout trayse."
"Nay, þou hast non," seis he · "for certeyn soþe,   625

ȝe han be fastned wiþ hem · þat ferden wiþ luitel."

"Tel me what is þin · and what hit signefyes?"

And he tolde hire a-non · trewely him-seluen,   628

And heo rikenede a-ȝeyn · radly and sone,

Also redili as he · and wonder he hedde.

¶ "I schal seiȝe þe, Ioseph · for certeyn soþe,

hou I tok cristendom · and in what tyme.   632

while my moder lyuede · heo hedde an vuel longe,

And souȝte in-to diuerse studes · and mihte haue non
    hele.

¶ þenne wonede an hermite · faste bi-syde ;

Semely vppon a day · þidere we souhten ;   636

Heo bad þis hermyte · he scholde hire hele sende.

¶ 'I am sinful as þou,' he seis · 'I mai þe non graunte.'

¶ 'No mak þi preyere to him,' heo seis · 'þat þin hope
    is inne?'

¶ 'woldestou leeue vppon him,' he seis · 'I wolde þe
    bi-hote,   640

þat þou scholdest ben hol · ar þou henne eodest.'

¶ He made hire to knele a-doun · and a bok bradde,

Radde a gospel þer-on · and bad hire vp rise,

And heo was lihtned of hire euel · in a luytel stounde.

¶ þenne heo seide to me · 'douȝter ful deore,   645

woltou beo as I am · and on þis mon leue?'

And I wepte water warm · and wette my wonges,

And seide his hert was so hor · I had not on him leeue.

And he seide to me · 'douȝter, he is seirore,   649

þat þi moder has I-helet · nou in þis tyme,

þen I or þou · or out þat is formed.'

¶ And I tolde him a-ȝeyn · 'and he so feir weore   652

as my broþer is at home · I wolde on him leeue.'

¶ 'Sikerly, douȝter,' he seis · 'so may grace sende

þat þou miȝt seo him þi-self · ar þow henne seche.'

þEnne com Ihesu crist · so cler in him-seluen,   656
    aftur þe furste blusch · we ne miȝte him bi-holden,

Side notes:
She asks him what his faith is.

He finds she is a Christian.

Her mother had a sore disease.

She asked a hermit to pray for her.

The hermit made the mother kneel down,

and she was healed.

The daughter said she can only believe upon one

who is as fair as her own brother.

Jesus Christ appeared to her,

And a wynt and a sauor · whappede us vmbe,

we weore so wel of vr-self · we nuste what we duden.

He vsede of Goddes bord · & a writ brouhte,   660

and she was
converted ;
bi-tauȝte me and my moder · murily to holden ;

þus cristendom I tok · in þat ilke tyme."

¶ "whi hastou let so longe · þi lord þis lyf leden ?"

but dared not tell
her husband.
"Sire, forsoþe," heo seis · "syker I ne dorste,   664

He is so feol in him-self · for no þing be-knowen,

Bote herkene of god · whon he his grace sende.

¶ Hastou not herd þi-self · hou euel he was to torne ?"

The king returns,
Now þe kyng comes to sarras · and mony on him

    suwen ;   668

As sone as he com hom · I hete þe forsoþe,

He askede after a-non · nomeliche þeose tweyne,

[* Fol. 4c4 b,
col. 2.]
and blesses
Joseph's God.
Sette him on *his bed · and hem on eiþer syde.

"A! Ioseph," seiþ þe kyng · "soþe aren þi wordes, 672

þat þou toldest me furst · ȝor foundeour be blesset !"

¶ "Ho is þat ?" seis Seraphe · and [he] onswerde

    sone,

" he þat halp þe wiþ sound · fro þe seue knihtes"—

Tolde hem vche a poynt · þat þei wrouȝt haden ;   676

Hou he wuste þerof · wonder hem þouȝte.

A knight appears
who has lost an
arm.
Þenne com on fro þe fiht · þat foule was wemmed,

    was striken of þat on Arm · and bar hit in þat

    oþer.

¶ þen Ioseph asked þe kynges scheld · And bad þat

    mon knele,

                                  680

Evelak's shield
restores the arm.
þe arm helede a-ȝeyn · hol to þe stompe.

¶ þenne com Seraphe · and fullouȝt furst askes.

Joseph baptizes
Seraphe by the
name of Naciens.
In þe nome of þe fader · Ioseph him fulwede,

And calles him Naciens · and his nome tornde :   684

he was þe forme þat day · þat fongede trouþe.

¶ whon he Baptised was · þis oþere bi-heolden,

Heom þouȝte he leomede as liht · al on a lowe ;

¶ þei seȝen þe holy-gost · at his mouþ descenden,   688   The Holy Ghost descends on him.
And he speek þenne · þat bi-foren ne kneuȝ.

Þ Enne com he wiþ þe sore Arm · þat þorw þe grace
    was holpen ; .
In þe nome of þe fader · Ioseph him folwed,   The healed knight is
clepen him Cleomadas · and callen him after.   692   baptized as Cleomadas,
¶ þenne com þe kyng Eualac · and fullouht askes ;
In þe nome of þe fader · Ioseph him folwede,   and Evelak as Mordreins.
Called him Mordreyns · 'a lat mon' in trouþe.
¶ þen com þe folk · to Iosaphe so þikke,   696
He tok a basin of gold · in boþe two his hondes,
Vppon þe heiȝe triuite · he let water hiȝe,   Joseph baptizes 5000 others.
And hedde fulwed bi non · mo þen fyue þousend.
¶ þenn seis Iosaphe · þat Ioseph his fader   700
mot a-byden him · and dwelle þer stille,
¶ while þat he and Naciens gon · nouþer þei nusten,
forte cristene þe folk · and casten þe false.
¶ But þere an vnsely kyng · in prison hem caste,   704   A king puts Iosaphe in prison,
wiþ muche serwe to him-self · siker atte laste ;
¶ For þe kyng Mordreyns · com with such strengþe,   but Mordreins releases him.
forte liuere hem out · on lyue he lafte none.
¶ Siþen þei bi-tauȝten þe blod · twei burnes to holden,
And þei lenden of þe toun · and leuen lut þere.   709   Joseph's company leave Sarras.

The Lyfe of Joseph of Armathy.

[REPRINTED FROM THE BLACK-LETTER COPY
PRINTED BY WYNKYN DE WORDE.]

[The Lyfe of Joseph of Armathy.]

[Leaf 1.] ¶ Here after foloweth a treatyse taken out of a boke whiche somtyme Theodosius the Emperour founde in Iherusalem in the pretorye of Pylate of Ioseph of Armathy.[1]

[Leaf 2.] FOr asmoche as oftentymes grete doubtes & doubtefull thynges deceyueth the reders / therfore all doubtes sette a parte ye shall se dyuers thynges extracte of the veray true & probate assercyons of hystoryal men touchynge and concernynge thantyquytes of thonourable monastery of oure lady in Glastenburye. After the tyme that our sauyour Ihesu cryste was put vnto deth by passyon of the crosse & all thynges were fully complete whiche were wryten and spoken of hym by holy prophecye. That holy man Ioseph of Armathy came vnto Pylate and asked of hym the body of our sauyour Ihesu cryste / whan yᵉ body was graunted to hym he wrapped it in a fayre whyte clothe and interyd it in a tombe newely made where neuer man was buryed in / what tyme the Iewes had parfyte knowlege that this Ioseph had so worshypfully brought the body of cryst in erthe / they thought vtterly in theyr myndes and kest so also the meanes how they myght set handes vpon hym / & one named Nychodemus and many dyuers other yᵉ whiche were the veray true louers and iust aduocates of our sauyour fledde and kepte them secrete / excepte onely the sayd Ioseph & Nychodemus whiche full boldly presented them selfe & made rehersall vnto yᵉ Iewes vnder these wordes / what sholde moue you to be dyspleased wᵗ vs for asmoche as we haue buryed yᵉ body of Ihesu cryst / knowe ye full well sayd Ioseph & Nychodemus to yᵉ Iewes yᵗ yᵉ haue mysdone agaynst yᵉ ryghtfull

[1] Beneath is a cut of the crucifixion with "Ihesus nazarenus rex iudeorum" at the top, and bordered with foliage. The same cut is repeated on the back of the leaf.

man / ye cast ne thynke not in your myndes the grete benefytes he
hathe done and shewed to you ye haue for his grete goodnes crucy-
fyed hym & with a sharpe spere wounded hym. The Iewes herynge
those wordes set hande on Ioseph and closed hym in an house where
was no wyndowe / & annas & cayphas sealed the dore vpon the locke
and assygned and deputed certayne[1] men to kepe hym and watche
hym / and his felowe Nychodemus was let goo at lyberte. They intreated Ioseph soo vngoodly for as moche that he was the man that
desyred the body of Ihesu cryst / and was the pryncypall mouer and
begynner that y⁰ body was so worshypfully interyd & buryed / after
this was done vpon theyr sabbat daye they gaderyd them in a companye y⁰ chefe rulers of the temple and caste theyr myndes togyder
how & by what maner of dethe they myght destroye Ioseph & whan
they were all in fere[2] Annas and Cayphas were commaunded by
theym to present Ioseph for as moche as they had sealed y⁰ dore where
he was inclosed in & whan theyr seales were broken & the dore
opened Ioseph was gone. Than they sent out spyes to seke hym &
fynably he was founde in his owne cyte called Aramathya / & whan
they had redy tydynges & perfyte knowlege of it / bothe chefe rulers
& all the comynalte of the Iewes inioyed gretely & thanked y⁰ verray
god of Israell y⁰ it was knowen where Ioseph was become whiche was
thus inclosed vnder kepynge warde and custodye. Thenne they
gadred in a multytude and they the whiche were pryncypalles and
heedes preposynge this questyon and sayd what meanes myghte we
fynde that we myght craftely haue Ioseph vnto vs and so for to
speke with hym. Thenne they *concluded generally that an [* Leaf 3.]
epystle sholde be wryten vnto hym / and this was the effecte of the
lettre. Ioseph peace be with the and with all thy company. Nowe
we knowe full well that we haue full greuously offended god and
the / therfore we praye the vouchsaue too come vnto vs that we
maye comen with the for we meruaylle gretely how thou was taken
out of the place in y⁰ whiche thou was putte / we knowlege ourselfe
vnto the that we haue malygned sore agayn the / wherfore almyghty
god hathe delyuered y⁰ that our wycked counseyll and vnhappye
mynde myght not hurte the / therfore worshyppefull Ioseph whiche

---

[1] *Printed* cretayne.   [2] i.e. *in-fere* = together.

arte well beloued amonge all people / peace be w^t the. Thenne this epystle made and wryten they chose seuen persones amonge theym all whiche were the best and moost synguler frendes that Ioseph had & sayd vnto theym / whan ye go forth take your way in to Aramathia vnto Ioseph & grete hym well in our behalue and take vnto hym this our epystle / whan ye seuen persones electe & chosen had theyr full answer with theyr lettre delyuered anone they came to ye cyte of Aramathya where Ioseph was and full louyngely salued hym shewynge theyr comynge & the cause gyuynge vnto hym y* epystle which receyued them full curteysly / and whan he had ouer-loked the lettre and knewe the effecte thenne he sayd these wordes. Blessyd be my lorde god of Israell whiche hathe delyuered and saued me that my blode hath not be shed nor I destroyed / blessed be my lorde god the whiche hathe kepte me vnder his wynges. Thenne Ioseph in token of loue & peace kyssed the .vii. persones whiche were sente in message vnto hym and full kyndely hadde them in to his house. And vpon the nexte daye after he toke his asse and walkynge kepte them company vnto Iherusalem. And whan the Iewes herde of his comynge they wente agaynst hym and in their metynge sayd with one voyce peace be in thy comynge fader Ioseph / and he resaluted theym vnder this maner and sayd. Peace be with you and amonge you all and there they kyssed hym all / thenne Nychodemus receyued hym in to his house and made hym a grete dyner / vpon a daye whan the Iewes were gadered togyder Annas and Cayphas sayd vnto Ioseph / shewe thou now before ye god of Israell & openly declare vnto vs suche thynges as we shall examyn the of for as moche as it is not vnknowen that we were sore greued for by cause thou lettest bury the body of Ihesu cryste and therupon we enclosed the in a preuy house and the morowe we sent to haue spoken with the and myght not fynde the / wherfore we meruaylled gretely and were sore affrayed of it how this myghte be vnto this tyme that we se the nowe / therfore whyles thou arte pre-sente certefye vs verely howe this mater was brought that thou was thus secretely conueyed awaye. Ioseph dydayned not to gyue theym answere but sayd vnto theym boldely. What tyme ye closed me in that house on godefrydaye the morowe vpon whiche is the sabbate

daye in the mydnyghte whan I was besy in my prayers to desyre god
to be my helpe and socour / sodeynly in ye meane tyme ye house
that I was in was taken vp by ye foure angles.   And I sawe Ihesus
bryghter thenne *ony lyght that euer I sawe afore and for [* Leaf 4.]
grete fere I fell downe to the erthe / thenne he toke me by the
hande frome the grounde and wyped my face with a rose and kyssed
me and sayd vnto me be not aferde Ioseph loke vpon me and knowe
thou full well that I am he.   Thenne loked I vp and called hym
mayster Helyas supposynge that he hadde ben Hely the prophete /
thenne he spake vnto me and sayd I am not Hely but I am Ihesus
whose boody thou letest be buryed / thenne for by cause I was som-
dele doubtfull of it I sayd vnto hym yf thou be he shewe me y^e
tombe wherin I layde the.   Thenne he toke me by ye hande and
broughte me vnto the place where I interyd hym.   Furthermore he
shewed me the clothe in ye whiche I wrapped his body and also the
sudarye that I bounde his hede withall.   Thenne these thynges seen
I knewe well that it was Ihesus and I honoured hym as my dutye
was recytynge these wordes. Blessyd be he that is come in the name
of god.   Thenne he toke me by the hande and soo ledde me in
myn house in the Cyte of Aramathya & sayd vnto me reste thou
here peacybly these fortye dayes go not forth frome thy house.   And
I shall goo vnto my dyscyples that hath grete luste for to se me.
And this sayd and done. Ihesus vanysshed awaye.   Thenne after
these fortye dayes were hole and fullye complete Ioseph of Aramathya
aboue reherced stedfastly fyxed his mynde in the feruente loue of the
fayth / gaue hym selfe to the dyscyplyne and doctryne of saynt
Phylyp the appostle of our blessyd lorde Ihesu Cryste.   And whan
that he was suffycyently instructe in his lore and techynge /
bothe he and his sone Iosephes receyued of saynt Phylyp the
holy sacrament of baptysme / and after that Ioseph was sent vpon
a message frome saynt Iohan the appostle & euangelyst from ephesye
vnto the gloryous moder of Ihesu cryste oure lady and also after that
was presente with saynt Phylyp and other dyscyples what tyme that /
that gloryous vyrgyn was assumpte in to heuen.   And as many
thynges as euer he herde and sawe of oure lorde Ihesu cryste and of
his blessyd moder oure lady saynt Mary / he shewed theym and

preched theym in dyuerse regyons and places and conuerted moche
people vnto the crysten fayth and baptysed them.   And at the last
.xv. yere after the gloryous assumpcyon of our blessyd lady he toke
his sone Iosephes with hym and wente to saynt Phylyp in to
Fraunce and consequently as it is wryten in a boke called Graall
Ioseph of Aramathia whiche buryed the body of oure lorde Ihesu
cryste after y^t he was baptysed of the holy man saynt Phylyp the
appostle came in to grete Brytayn whiche was promysed to hym and
hys yssue & he brought with hym his wyfe and his sone Iosephes
whome our sauyoure before that tyme hadde made a bysshop and
consecrate hym in a Cyte called Sara / & there came with hym syxe
hondred persones of men and women and mo / & the men made a
solempne vowe for to lyue chastely from theyr wyues vnto the tyme
they hadde entered in to grete Brytayne and all the nombre brake
this vowe except .xxxvii. whiche were commaunded by our sauyour
to passe ouer ye se saylynge vpon the shyrte of Iosephes and soo
[* Leaf 5.] came to londe * vpon Ester euen in the mornyñge / ye resydue
of them for as moche as they were penytent and sory for the trans-
gressyon of theyr vowe at thynstaunce & prayer also of Ioseph were
brought ouer in a vessell whiche kynge Salamon craftely had made
to contynue and dure vnto crystes tyme / and ye same daye that
theyr companye came vnto londe vpon Iosephs shyrte they applyed
vnto londe in ye same vessell whiche god had prouyded for theym
whiche were gyded by a duke of Medor named Natianiis whome
Ioseph baptysed before in the cyte of Sara / and with theym came
also the kynge of the same cyte called Mordrams to whome almyghty
god after that appered & shewed to hym his syde handes & feet
perysshed with the spere and nayles / and whan the kynge Mordrams
sawe that he was moued with compassyon and sayd.   O my lorde
god what man was so bolde and so presumptuous thus to dele with
y^e / our sauyour answered to hym agayne and sayd.   The false
kynge of Northwales hath this wyse done with me whiche hathe
put my seruaunt Ioseph of Aramathya with his company in pryson
and full vnkyndly denyeth them theyr lyuynge for by cause they
shewed & preched my name in his realme / therfor sayd almyghty god vnto mordrams / gyrde the with thy swerde aboute

thy myddell and goo with all hast possyble vnto that partyes
and take vengeau*n*ce vpon the tyraunt & delyuer my seruauntes
oute of pryson & daunger / whan y⁰ kynge awoke of his slepe
he was full glade of that vysyon shewed vnto hym and so set his
realme & his housholde in good waye & toke a grete company with
hym & toke his Iourney and as god was his guyde he came vnto the
place where the kynge of Northwales the tyraunt was and commaunded hym he sholde promytte and suffre the seruauntes of almyghty god to passe out of pryson and to be at lyberte / the tyraunt
wolde not in no wyse condescende vnto kynge Mordrams commaunde-
ment / but with grete indygnacyon charged hym shortely without
delaye to voyde out of his londe whan kynge Mordrams herde this
langage he came fyersly vpon hym with his company and with[1] duke
Naciamis aboue sayd & with condygne and Iuste vengeaunce slewe
hym / thenne this done kynge Mordrams wente vnto the pryson
where that vnhappye kynge hadde Ioseph and his company in holde /
& with grete Ioye brought them forth and shewed vnto them the
vysyon made vnto hym of god and theyr delyuerynge thenne all
they in grete myrthe thanked god hertely. Thenne kynge Mordrams[2]
gaue the realme & kyngedome of Northwales with the appertenence
vnto one called Celydomus sone vnto duke Nacyanus and gaue hym
also to be his wyfe Labell the kynges doughter of Persye whiche
Labell the sayd Celydomus with helpe and socoure of his fader
hadde before with grete dyffyculte conuerted vnto Crystes fayth
whose doubt[y]e and meruaylous actes be wryten in y⁰ bokes named
Grall aboue reherced.

¶ Thus endeth the lyfe of Ioseph of Armathy Enpry[n]ted at
    London in Flete strete at the sygne of the sonne by me Wynkyn
    de Worde.[3]

---

[1] *Printed* and with and duke.   [2] *Printed* Mordradms.
[3] On the sixth and last leaf is a cut of Jesse lying on the ground, from
whom issues a genealogical tree, representing the kings of Judah, and in the
midst of them the Virgin Mary, holding the infant Jesus in her arms, as
deriving her descent from Jesse. On the back of the leaf is Wynkyn de
Worde's common tripartite device. See Herbert's Ames; vol. i., p. 232. On
p. 233 is the remark—" This and the eleven preceding articles are among Bp.
More's books in the Public Library, Cambridge "—a remark which has reference to the very copy used for producing this reprint.

33

[Fol. lviii.]

¶ De Sancto Ioseph Ab arimathia.

[Reprinted from " The Kalendre of the New Legende of Englande,"
printed by Richard Pynson, A.D. 1516.]

WHen our lorde Ihesu Criste was crucefyed, Ioseph Ab
Arimathia asked of Pylate the bodye of our Lorde / and
leyde it in a clene Sendell / and put it in a Sepulcre that no man
had ben buryed in, as the Euangelyst[es] testifie, & the Iues heryng
therof put hym in a derke Pryson that had no wyndowe, and Annas
and Cayphas locked the dores, and after, when they had thought to
haue put hym to deth, they sent *for hym to the pryson ; [* Fol. lviii b]
and before theyr commynge on the saterday at nyght, our lord
apperyd to hym with a great bryghtnes as he was in prayer, & foure
aungellys lyfted vp þᵉ house that he was in, and our Lorde sayd to
hym, " I am Ihesus whom thou hast buryed " / and then Ioseph
sayd, " lord, if thou be he, shewe me the monument that I put the
in ; " and our lord toke hym by the hande and ledde hym to the
sepulcre, & fro thens he brought hym into his house at Arimathe ;
after, the Iues sent for hym, & asked of hym howe he came out of
pryson ; and he tolde them as byfore apperyth / and then they let
hym goo / & he became disciple to seynt Phylyp, & of hym he and
his sone Iosefes were baptised ; and he was a messenger fro Ephese
bytwyxt seynt Iohñ Euangelyst and our Ladye, and was at her
departynge with other disciples ; he was a Constaunte precher of the
worde of god as he had herde of our lorde and of our Lady, and con-
uertyd moche people ; after, he, with his sone Iosefes, went into
Fraunce to seynt Phylyp / and he sent Ioseph and his sone with .x.

other into Brytayne / & at last they came to a place then called
Inswytryñ, nowe called glastonburye / and thyse verses be made at
Glastonburye of theyr commynge.   Intrat Aualloniam duodena
caterua viror*um* / flos Arimathie Ioseph est prim*us* eor*um* / Iosefes
ex Ioseph genit*us* p*a*trem cōmitat*ur* / hiis aliisq*ue* decem ius glastonie
propriat*ur*.   And after, by monycion of the Archaungell gabryell,
they made a Churche or oratory of o*ur* Lady / & there they lyued a
blessed lyf in vigylles, fastingz, & prayers.   And two kynges, seynge
theyr blessid lyfe, though th[e]y were paynymes, gaue to eucryche of
theym a hyde of lande, whiche to this day be called the .xii. hydes /
and there they dyed ; and Ioseph was buryed nygh to the sayd
oratory.[1]

[1] The title of the first part of the book from which this extract is made
runs thus—" Here begynneth the Kalandre of the newe legende of Englande "
—beneath which is a cut representing the Crucifixion.   The book contains
three different treatises, the second being " The lyfe of seynt Birgette," and the
third " A deuote Boke compylyd by mayster Walter Hylton to a deuoute man
in temperall estate," &c.   The colophon to the first part is—" ¶ Thus endyth
the Kalendre of the new Legende of Englande / Emprynted to the honour of
the gloriouse Seyntz therin conteyned by Richarde Pynson / prynter to our
Souerayne lorde Kynge Henry the .viii."   Beneath this is the printer's device
No. 4.   The colophon to the second part gives us the date 1516.   See the description in Herbert's Ames, vol. i. p. 261.

¶ Here begynneth the lyfe of Joseph of Armathia.

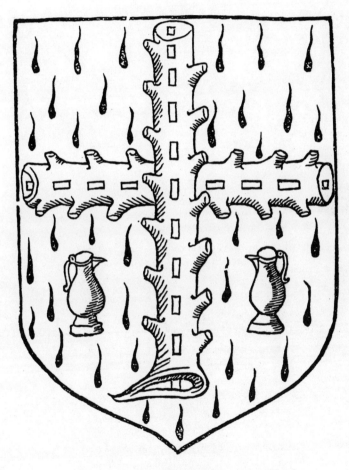

[*Reprinted from the black-letter copy printed
by Richard Pynson, A.D. 1520.*]

[¶ Here begynneth the lyfe of Joseph of Armathia.]

[See title on p. 35.]

I Hesu, the royall ruby, moost hye of renowne,
  Rested in Mary *the* mayde / for her humylyte ;
And fro *the* realme of rightwysnes / descended down
To take the meke clothyng / of our humanyte.　　4

[leaf 1, back]
Jesus became incarnate,

The .v. welles of pyte to open, Adam restored he
On the crosse, & for vs shedde / his precyous blode ;
There was the boke vnclapsed / of perfyte charyte,
With Longis spere smyten / hangyng on the rode.　　8

and shed His blood, being smitten by Longinus' spear.

His precyous body / on the crosse beyng deed,
Sore it greued his dyscyples / euery-chone ;
And in the olde bokes, as we rede,
That amonge all other there was one,　　12
His hert was perysshed *with* very compassyon.
His name called Ioseph / the lorde of Aromathy,
He went to pylate & full humbly desyred hym
To haue the body of Ihesu / hym for to bury.　　16

His disciples were grieved.

Joseph of Arimathea asks for His body.

And pylate graunted hym all his askyng,
Than ioseph retourned / *with* countenaunce demure,
And prayed Nycodymus / to go with hym
For to take downe / our lordes precyous body.　　20
So Ioseph layde Ihesu / to rest in his sepulture,
And wrapped his body / in a clothe called sendony ;
Ryche was it wrought, *with* golde & sylke full pure,
Ioseph of a mayd it bought / in Aromathy cyte.　　24

Nicodemus and Joseph take Jesus down.

Joseph wraps Christ's body in "sendony."

But yet whan Ioseph Ihesu downe toke,

The syde *that* the wound was on / lay to his brest ;
The colde blode / that was at our lordes herte rote
Fell within Iosephes sherte / & lay on his chest.   28

Truly as holy scripture sayth / there dyde it rest
At the holy place / aboue his stomake,

And whan our lorde / in the sendony was drest,
Thys blode in two cruettes / Ioseph dyd take.   32

The Iewes herd say / *that* Ioseph Ihesu had buryed,
They thought *that* Nycodemus & he shulde repent ;

The[y] went to pylat / & sayd they were greued,
Ioseph & Nycodemus for them both they sent.   36
Than came they to pylat, to knowe all his entente,
& sayd they had buryed ihesu / as he gaue them leue ;

"I-wys," sayd all the iewes / that there were present,
"He shall curse *the* tyme / that his body dyd remeue."

"Why," sayd Ioseph, " iesu was goddes owne sonne,

That ye bounde lyke a thefe / & hyng on the rode ;
Also to *the* hert with a sharpe spere / ye hym stonge,
& with .iii. nayles made hym shede his giltles blode.
I wote well, he neuer dyd yll / but euermore gode ; 45

He made *the* blynde to se / & heled some of lepry ;
He resed Lazarus / also / by his worde,
This is true," sayd Ioseph / " ye knowe as well as I."

The Iues put Ioseph / in a stronge prison of stone,   49
In that darke house / by hym-selfe he lay.
Lyght he coude not se / for wyndowe had it none,
The[y] locked the dore / and than went theyr way. 52

Cayphas and Anna / of that kept the kay,
And sealed the dore / also / they thought to be sure ;
For " Ioseph shulde dye" / playnly dyd they say,
But pacyently all theyr truble / dyd he endure.   56

Than Ihesu Christ / at his resurrection   [leaf 2, back]
To Ioseph apered / about hye mydnyght,
And rered all the foure corners / of that pryson,
The walles he susteyned / by his great myght.   60
Ioseph. that / meruayled / seyng so great a lyght,
A full precious water / our lorde threwe in his face,
Before that hour / he sawe neuer so swete a syght.
" Who is there ?" sayd Ioseph / " art thou Elyas ?" 64

Christ appears to Joseph, and raises his prison.

Joseph sees a great light.

He asks if it is Elias.

Our lorde spake to Ioseph / & bad hym nat fere,
He sayd. "aryse" / & toke hym vp by the hande ;
" I am Ihesu / whom thou buryed in the sepulture."
" If thou be" / sayd Ioseph / " that here doth stande,
Gyue me the rychest / treasour / of this lande,   69
The clothe / that is called the Sendony."
Ihesu led hym to the sepulture / & there it fonde ;
" Holde, ioseph," sayd ihesu / "*that* couerture of my
     body."   72

Christ reveals Himself to Joseph,

and gives him the cloth in which He was buried.

There ihesu bad ioseph to his owne place wende,
And sayd, " kepe thou thy house / dayes fully forty ;
Farwell," sayd our lorde, " Ioseph, my frende,
Where euer thou becom / peace be with the ;   76
I go to my disciples / that longe after me."
Ioseph wept for ioy / that was of yeres olde,
Saynge / " o Ihesu, worshypped may thou be ;
For thy grace, I haue spyed / is better than golde." 80

Christ tells Joseph to stay at home 40 days.

Joseph weeps for joy.

Ioseph kept his house, as our lorde bad,
And on the morowe cayphace went to the pryson ;
No body he there founde ; than was he full sad.   83
" Where is Ioseph ?" sayd anne, " I trowe he be gon !
I marueyle," he sayd ; " the scales were hole eche one,
And yet he out of the house is gone ! "
For wo they all wyst nat what to done,   87
Sayeng, " he that connayed hym was a false felone."

Caiaphas cannot find Joseph.

Annas says he is gone.

[leaf 3]

They hear that
Joseph is in
Arimathea,

So worde they had that in Armathya cyte
Ioseph was / than sent they to hym gretyng
By theyr letters made full craftely,
Him lowly prayeng that theyr writing   92
He wolde[1] ouer-se, and as [touchyng] any thyng
That was done to hym, they were wo therfore ;

and pray him to
come to
Jernsaiem.

And prayed to Ioseph, his louers he wolde bryng,
For they wolde be frendes with hym for euermore.   96

This mater to shorten, Ioseph thyder Went,

Joseph tells them
how he was
released,

And shewed them how theyr lorde delyuered hym
Out of the pryson ; " suche grace god me sent."
" Well," sayd the Iewes, " we meruayle of one thyng,
How he gate [thee] out with all his connyng."   101

and how Christ
lifted the prison
off the ground.

Ioseph sayd, " he lyfted the house fro the grounde."
They sayd, " by what crafte was it hanging,
That it fell nat in sonder, but stode styll sounde ? "

Joseph reminds
them of the
wonders at the
Crucifixion,

" Well," sayd Ioseph, " this was a great wonder,   105
Whan the sharpe spere to his hart was pyght,
To se great rockes and stones breke a-sonder,
The sonne darked & withdrewe his lyght.   108
The erthe trymbled by his great myght ;
All these were maruaylous," sayd Ioseph than ;

when the dead
bodies rose.

" Deed bodyes in theyr graues were sene with sight ;[2]
Wherfore I dare say, he is very god and man."   112

[leaf 3, back]

Now here how Ioseph came into englande ;
But at that tyme it was called brytayne.

Joseph was 15
years with Mary,

Than .xv. yere with our lady, as I vnderstande,
Ioseph wayted styll / to serue hyr he was fayne ;   116

but after her
Assumption went
to France with St
Philip.

So after hyr assumpcyon, the boke telleth playne,
With saynt Philyp he went into fraunce,
His sonne and his wyfe to serue god with payne,
Fayne for to folowe vertuous gouernaunce.   120

[1] *Printed* holde.   [2] *Printed* sihgt.

Ioseph had a sonne whose name was Iosephas,
That our lorde a bysshop dyd consecrate,
A vertuous lyuer the boke sayth that he was,
Phylip bad them go to great brytayn fortunate. 124
So to the see they went, of ioye seperate,
For of them there were .v. C. & mo
In that company, bothe erly and late,
Taryeng for passage / togyder forto go. 128

His son,
Josephas, was
made bishop by
Christ.

500 of his
company set out
to go to Britain.

A shyp they toke, as I vnderstande,
And passed without peryll ouer the salt streme ;
Into the hauen they all aryued to lande,
But yet of brytayne they sayled theyr course clene. 132
They fortuned to a countre of a tyraunt kene,
Called wales, there was a kyng that tyme ;
They landed all, as the boke telleth, on an ester euyn,
xxxi. yere after the passyon, about the houre of nyne.

They take ship,

but land in
Wales on Easter
eve, 31 years after
the Passion.

Whan the kyng knewe that they dyd lande, 137
He toke Ioseph and all his felowes truly,
And put them in pryson great and strong ;
Than they all prayed to god almyghty, 140
And he herde theyr prayers lyghtly,
That they were delyuered in short space ;
He thought his seruauntes sholde nat in peryll lye,
Than he sent them confort by his great grace. 144

The king puts
Joseph and his
fellows in prison.

[leaf 4]

God condescends
to deliver them.

Our lorde apered to a kyng in the west,
That named was Mordrayous in dede,
Bydding hym for to make hym prest,
With all his myght in to wales to spede ; 148
Sayng, "there be my seruauntes, that of helpe nede,
Go thou theder and bere thy[1] swerde in thy hande ;
That proude kyng that me doth nat drede,
Thou shalt hym ouercome and all his lande." 152

Christ appears
to king
Mordrayous,

and tells him to
go to Wales.

[1] *Printed* they.

King Mordrayous
obeys,

Than the kyng, after his vysion sene,
Thought in hast his deuer to do ;
So vp he rose in the mornyng,
All his lordes he called hym to.   156
He sayd, "in to wales in dede must I go ;

and prepares to
go to Wales.

Now thyder wyll I hye me with all my myght ;
God to me appered, and bad me do so,
Agayne the prince of that countre for to fight."   160

He makes over
his own kingdom
to a lord.

In all hast he dysposed his householde,
And to a lorde he toke the realme to gouerne,
To delyuer goddes seruauntes he sayd he wolde ;
" I knowe no maner man that shall me werne."   164
In his iourney he hyed, he thought not to turne,
Tyll he came to the place there Ioseph was.

He burns some
Welsh towns,
and frightens the
king.

Many a towne in wales dyd he burne,
The prynce of that countre herd therof in space ;   168

[leaf 4, back]

And to Mordrayous he sent a messangere,

The king of
Wales submits,

Prayng hym to come in with peace.
He sayd, " this lande is poore, therfore I hym fere,
Besechyng his goodnesse this stryfe to sease ;   172
And I wyll hym gyue a lady perelesse,

and offers him his
daughter, named
Labell.

Myn owne doughter, by name called Labell,
Precyously arayed in cloth of rychesse :"—
He bad the messangere all this vnto hym tell.   176

A messenger
comes to
Mordrayous,

Than went the messangere vnto Mordrayous,
And sayd all, as is before tolde :—
" Syr kyng, my lorde the prayeth to be gracious
Vnto him, and not so fyerse and bolde ;   180
And ye shall haue his doughter with plentie of golde,

saying that
Joseph shall be
released.

With all the prysoners that in his pryson be,
Ioseph & his felowes, both yong and olde."
Than sayd Mordrayous, " he shall haue peace with me."

On a day these kynges togeder both dyd mete,
Mordrayous toke Labell to his wyfe ;
Eche saluted other with wordes swete,
And loued togyder the terme of theyr lyfe. 188
For Mordrayous was doughty with swerd & knyfe,
That all landes nere hym dyd dowt.
Ioseph was delyuered from daunger blyfe,
With his felawes, all the hole rowt. 192

Mordrayous marries Labell.

Joseph is released.

Than hyther into brytayne Ioseph dyd come,
And this was by kyng Aueragas dayes ;
So dyd Ioseph and also Iosephas his sonne,
With many one mo, as the olde boke says. 196
This kynge was hethen & lyued on fals layes,
And yet he gaue to Ioseph au[i]lonye,
Nowe called Glastenbury, & there he lyes ;
Somtyme it was a towne of famous antyquyte.[1] 200

Joseph comes to Britain in the days of Arviragus,

[leaf 5]

who gives to Joseph Avilion, now called Glastonbury.

There Ioseph lyued with other hermyttes twelfe,
That were the chyfe of all the company,
But Ioseph was the chefe hym-selfe ;
There led they an holy lyfe and gostely. 204
Tyll, at the last, Ihesu the mighty,
He sent to Ioseph thaungell gabryell,
Which bad hym, as the wrytyng doth specify,
Of our ladyes assumpcyon to bylde a chapell. 208

Here Joseph and 12 hermits lived.

Gabriel tells Joseph to build a chapel to Our Lady.

So Ioseph dyd as the aungell hym bad,
And Wrought there an ymage of our lady ;
For to serue hyr great deuocion he had,
And that same ymage is yet at Glastenbury, 212
In the same churche ; there ye may it se.
For it was the fyrst, as I vnderstande,
That euer was sene in this countre ;
For Ioseph it made wyth his owne hande. 216

Joseph does so.

Our Lady's image is still at Glastonbury.

[1] *Printed* autyquyte.

He also made a
crucifix,

The rode of northdore of london also dyd he make,
Moche lyke as our lorde was on the rode done ;
For this Ioseph fro the crosse hym dyd take.
And loke howe a man may make by proporcion   220
A deed ymage lyke a quycke, by cunnynge ;

now the "Rood
of Northdoor."

So lyke the rode of northdore Iesu henge deed,
For Ioseph made it nere semyng
Vnto our lorde enclynynge his heed.   224

[leaf 5, back]

Than Ioseph there abode, prechyng the fayth,

Joseph dies.

Tyll by the course of nature he dyed ;
Thus the olde boke recordeth and sayth,

He is buried at
Glastonbury,

But in dede his body at Glastenbury doth abyde.   228
Our lorde for hym well doth prouyde,

where he is
sought by many a
thousand.

Likely there to be sought with many a .M. ;
The name of Glastenbury wyll sprede full wyde
To men & women of many a straunge lande.   232

In the 18th year
o' our king
Henry,

By whose prayer god sheweth many myrakyll,
Proued the .xviii. yere of henry our kyng ;
In doltyng parysshe, there was sicke longe whyle

two women of
Dolting parish
were healed of the
pestilence,

Two yonge women of the pestelence, lamentyng,   236
Which passed the cure of men in eche thynge.
Theyr prayer makyng to ioseph of Aramathye,

and offered at
Glastonbury on
St Simon's day.

So begau to recouer, & brought theyr offryng
On Symone day & Iude vnto Glastenbury.   240

Many miracles
have happened
there.

And syth god there hath shewed many a myrakyl.
I lacke tyme & season all to expresse ;
But yet all that do vysyte that holy habytakyll,
It is euer lyke newe to them that call in distresse. 244

His body has
lain there 400
[? 1400] years.

Four C. yere ago / the boke bereth wytnes,
So longe there hath rested that holy body ;
And nowe pleaseth it god, of his goodnesse,
Great myracles for hym to worke, as ye may se.   248

Many be there holpen through our lordes myght ;
A chylde of welles raysed fro deth without dout.
Lame ar there heled, the blynde restored to sight ;
One that had the fransy to his wytte was brought. 252
The vykary of welles, that thyder had sought,
On the tenth day, that many men dyd se,
Where .iiii. yere afore he stande nor go mought,
Released he was of part of his infyrmyte.　　256

There is continuaunce of grace, as it is shewed
On a woman of banwell, the wyfe of Thomas Roke,
whyche was tempted by the fende & greatly styred ;
With hyr husbandes knyues she cut hyr throte,　260
And doutlesse, as true men do report,
She slewe hyr selfe, so greuous was the wounde.
For wo hyr husband wyst not whether to resort,　263
Whan he sawe hyr all blody & his own knife found.

This wofull man, seynge his wyfe thus lye,
Whiche with his knyfe had done that wofull dede,
Vnto his neyghbours he cryed full pyteously,
Hym for to helpe in that tyme of nede.　　268
The wounde to sewe fast he began to spede,
Besechynge our lorde and holy Ioseph,
This woman to saue, and so hertely prayed,
That anone after she began to drawe brethe.　272

And they yet say, that the stytches brake,
That the flesshe / closed, and that was wonder ;
She was confessed / hoseled / eneled, and spake,
Therfore, good men, this in your myndes ponder ;　276
yet lyueth, & in the .ix. day of apryl came she thyder,
And went before the honourable procession.
The same knyfe she offred vp all blody there ;　279
Now thanked be god & Ioseph, she is hole & sounde.

The .ix. day of Aprill, Iohñ Lyght, gentylman,

Dwellynge besyde Ilchester at lyghtes care,

His wyfe had vpon her a feuer quartayn,

By the space of two yere vexed gretly ;   284

No medycyne nor phisyke *that* coude do her remedy ;

[She prayed to Ioseph to hele her of her payne],[1]

And promysed thyder her offrynge deuontly,

Than was she delyuered of her dyscase certayne.   288

The tenth daye of Apryll, that was than sonday,

A chylde was smyten with a plage all deed,

And to euery mannes syght an houre so he lay.

His moder hertely to sent Ioseph prayed,   292

And bowed[2] her offryng, in her hert sore afrayed.

The chylde recouered and had his hele,

And on saynt marke daye there they offred,

Hole and sounde ; no herme dyde he fele.   296

The .xv. day of Apryll one Robert Browne,

Of yeuell, that at ylchester was prysoner,

He was delyuered by proclamatyon,

And went to gader his fees for the kepar.   300

The prysoner about his legge had a fetter ;

He prayed ioseph to helpe him, as he was not gilty,

And sodenly the fetters sprange fro hym there,

In myddes of *the* market-place of Glastenbury.   304

Iohñ Gyldon, gentylman, of port melborne,

The syde of his mouth was drawen to his eare ;

His lyft syde and his arme was benome,

That he of his lyfe stode in great fere ;   308

Speke coude he nat nor hymselfe stere.

He prayed to Ioseph, promysyng his offryng,

So of his sykenes he was delyuered clere,

Saue onely of an hurte in his lefte arme.   312

---

[1] A line omitted. Supplied from conjecture.   [2] *For* vowed ?

The .xx. day of apryll, Iohñ popes wyfe of comtone,   *The 20th of*
April, the wife of
Had a yong chylde, that was taken sodenly,   *John Pope, of*
Comton, had a
And so contynued and coude not be holpen ;   *sick child.*
His moder prayed to god and Ioseph deuoutly,   316
Her offrynge promysed, than founde she remedy.
The chylde recouered, & had his lymmes at wyll.   *He recovered.*
Lo ! ye well dysposed people, here may ye se,
That there is nothynge to god impossyble.   320

yonge walter sergaunt, dwellynge in Pylton,   *The child of*
Walter Sergeaunt,
His chylde in the pestylence was in Ieopardy,   *of Pilton,*
was nearly dead.
And sore panged that he myght not meue hym,
So that to theyr syght he appered deed veryly.   324
This wofull moder, as the neyghbours testefy,
Prayed to Ioseph and of the chylde the mesure,
And promysed to do her offrynge truly ;
Than shortly after the chylde dyde recure.   328   *He recovered.*

Also Alys, wyfe to Walter benet, dwellyng in welles,   *Alice, wife of*
Walter Bennet of
Infect with the frenche pockes a yere and more,   *Wells, was quite*
lame.
And doutlesse, as her owne neyghbours telles,
Her fete were so paynfull and sore,   332
That go coude she not but as she was bore.
Thyder was she brought in-to the chapell,   *She left her stilts*
in the chapel.
Verely she was heled, and lefte her styltes thore,
And on her fete wente home resonably well.   336

Iohñ Abyngdons wyfe, of welles, had a sykenesse,   *[leaf 7, back]*
Moost paynfull with a sore called a fistula ;   *The wife of John*
Abingdon, of
So long it[1] contynued that she laye spechelesse,   *Wells, had a*
fistula.
And her lymbes dyde rotte, truly they do say,   340
So that with a knyfe the peces were cut away.
At last she thought she had sene Ioseph in pycture,
How he toke god fro the crosse, & to hym dyde pray,
Her for to hele, and than began she to recure.   344   *She was healed.*

---

[1] *Printed* is.

All the myracles to shewe it were to longe,
There is many mo full great *that* I do not reherse.
As pestylence, purpyls, and agonys strong,   347
With megrymes also, & men *that* haue lyen specheles.
And this I knowe well, both in prose, ryme, & verse,
Men loue nat to rede an over longe thyng ;
Therfore I entende this mater to short & sease,
I pray you all to marke well the endynge.   352

ye pylgrymes all, gyue your attendaunce
Saynt ioseph there to serue with humble affectyon,
At Glastenbury for to do hym reuerence ;
Lyft vp your hertes with goostly deuocyon,   356
Therwith conceyuyng this brefe compylacyon ;
Though it halte in meter of eloquence,
All thyng is sayd vnder correctyon,
And wryten to do holy Ioseph reuerence.   360

ye lettred, that wyll haue more intellygence
Of the fyrst foundacyon of Ioseph there,
The olde bokes of Glastenbury shall you ensence,
More plainly to vnderstande this forsayd matere.   364
To you shall declare the hole cronycle clere,
Wryten full truly with a notable processe.
Make ye no doute, nor be not in fere,
As olde clerkes therof bereth wytnesse.   368

Sothely Glastenbury is *the* holyest erth of england,
Rede saynt Dauydes lyfe, and there may ye se,
That our lorde it halowed with his owne hande ;
For Dauyd by myracle proued it, parde.   372
Chryst made through his handes two holes truely,
Than went Dauyd, and his masse began ;
And, after sakeryng, the holes dyd shyt ; "a!" sayd he,
"This church was halowed by a better than I am !"

Great meruaylles men may se at Glastenbury,
One of a walnot tree that there dooth stande,
In the holy grounde called the semetory,   379
Harde by *the* place where kynge Arthur was founde.
South fro Iosephs chapell it is walled in rounde,
It bereth no leaues tyll the day of saynt Barnabe;
And than that tree, that standeth in the grounde,
Spredeth his leaues as fayre as any other tree.   384

There is at
Glastonbury a
walnut-tree near
Arthur's tomb,

which bears no
leaves till St
Barnabas day.

Thre hawthornes also, that groweth in werall,
Do burge and bere grene leaues at Christmas
As fresshe as other in May, whan *the* nightyngale
Wrestes out her notes musycall as pure as glas;   388
Of all wodes and forestes she is *the* chefe chauntres.
In wynter to synge yf it were her nature,
Iu werall she myght haue a playne place,
On those hawthornes to shewe her notes clere.   392

Three hawthorns
at Werrall bear
green leaves at
Christmas.

The nightingale
might sing there
at Christmas.

Lo, lordes, what Ihesu dooth in Ianuary,
Whan the great colde cometh to grounde;
He maketh the hauthorne to sprynge full fresshely.
Where as it pleaseth hym, his grace is founde;   396
He may loose all thing that is bounde.
Thankes be gyuen to hym that in heuen sytteth,
That floryssheth his werkes so on the grounde,
And in Glastenbury, *Quia mirabilia fecit.*   400

[leaf 8, back]

Jesus makes the
hawthorn bud in
January.

Thanks be to Him
who works
miracles at
Glastonbury.

50

¶ A praysyng to Joseph.

Praise to thee, O Joseph.

O Ioseph, sanctificate is thy fyrst foundation,
Thy parentycle may be praysed of vs all.
Armony syng with hertely Iubylacyon,
That causeth many sorowes fro theyr hertes fall,   404
Of creatures dysconsolate that there for grace call,
Lawdyng Ioseph with deuoute reuerence,

Here shall many find comfort.

As a principall place chosen of Christ moost speciall;
There shal thei fynde confort of Christes magnificence.

Hall, mighty giant!

Hayle, mighty gyaunt, heuen & erth thou dyde bere,
As bright as the mone that[1] Illumyneth the nyght;
Moche stronger than Sampson that had no pere;

Hall, fragrant flower!

Hayle, floure fragrant; it with thy great myght   412
Putteth fendes vnto flyght, and euery yll ayre,
From men that deuoutly do theyr dylygence
Here Ioseph to serue with offrynge or prayer,
Shall fynde confort of our lordes magnyficence.   416

Hall, Joseph, who didst bear the honey-comb on Good Friday.

Hayle, Ioseph, that bere the swete hony combe
On good friday, as holy scripture doth specyfie,
In thyn earme thou bere both the lyon & the lambe,

[leaf 9]

God and man in one humanyte.   420
In sepulture thou layd the myrrour of humylyte,

Thou didst bury the mirror of humility.

Bryghter than lucyfer in his resplendence,
After he had payed our raunsom and made vs fre
Of his great fauour, grace, and magnyfycence.   424

[1] Printed than.

Hayle, myghty balynger, chargcd with plenty,
Thou hast cast anker in the hauen of aduentere ;
O dentyous dyamonde, *the* destroyer of yll desteny,
As gay as euer was phebus in his golde spere ;   428
O noble Ioseph, the tyme of grace draweth nere.

Hail, mighty well-laden ship !

Hayle, myrre so precyous, dystroynge al pestelence ;
O royall gem, whome men shall seke full ferre,
Here to haue confort of our lordes magnyfycence.   432

Hail, precious myrrh, royal gem !

Heyle, tresour of Glastenbury moost imperyall,
In sauour smellynge swete as eglantyne ;
Now shall thy name flourysshe ouerall,
Ihesu for thy sake the bell of mercy doth rynge.   436
Great cause hath Englande *Laus deo* to synge,
God and Ioseph to prayse *with* all our dylygence,
That many men delyuereth out of mournynge,
By our lordes fauour, grace, & magnyfycence.   440

Hail, treasure of Glastonbury !

Great cause hath England to praise God.

O noble Ioseph, O ghostly phesycyon,[1]
By the is cured many a malady ;
Nat vsynge pylles / dregges / ne pocyon,
Ne other medecyne, yet doost thou remedy   444
To pockes / pestylence / and also frency,
And all maner of feuer, we so experyence ;
Thou helest Iaundes / goutes, and dropsyes
By our lordes fauour, grace, and magnyfycence.   448

Oh ghostly physician,

who dost use no pills ;

thou healest jaundice and gout.
[leaf 9, back]

Now, holy Ioseph, pray for vs to our lorde
To sende vs peas and perfyte charite,
And amonge the comyns welth and concorde,
And that our ryche men may vse lyberalyte,   452
Whiche than shall [wende] towarde the deyte,
Where aungelles to Ihesu do great reuerence ;
Vnto the whiche god bryng bothe you & me
Of his fauour, grace, and magnyfycence.   456

Joseph, pray for us !

May our rich men be liberal !

God bring us to heaven !

[1] *Printed* phecysron.

¶ Ioseph, serue dei omnipotentis, miserere mei malefactoris. Esto michi solamen in suspiriis,[1] continuum iuuamen in molestiis. Super id quod opto da remedium, & tollator eo quicquid dessonum (sic). Ioseph, discipule, da in futuris agenda facere, in non agendis vim hec resistere, in virtuosis vitam terminare, demum in celis tecum habitare.

versus. Sancte ioseph, *christi* discipule. *Responsorium.* Intercede *pro* nobis ad Iesum qui elegit te. Oremus.

DOmine iesu *christe*, cui *omnis* lingua confitetur, respice in nos seruos tuos & placare precibus tui dilecti discipuli ioseph : vt ipso intercedente mereamur in presentia habere peccati[2] remedium, & in futuro tue visionis dulcedinem. Qui viuis. &c.

¶ *Responsorium.* Serue dei, ioseph sanctissime, preces *nostras* clementer accipe, morbos cedes[3] & pestes remoue. Et si meremur iam penas luere, *christum* regem superne glorie non iratum sed blandum effice. *versus.* Vt cum ceperit mundum discernere & in dextris[4] oues reponere. Non ira. Oratio.

[lea. 10] OMnipotens, sempiterne deus, qui beatissimum ioseph famulum tuum tribuisti vnigeniti filii tui corpus exanime de cruce deponere : eique iusta humanitatis officia persoluere,[5] presta quesumus, vt qui eius memoriam deuote recolimus consuete misericordie tue senciamus auxilium. Per eundem dominum nostrum.

A   M   E   N.

¶ Imprinted at London in Fletestrete at the
sygne of the George / by Richard Pynson printer vnto the kinges noble
grace Anno. domini.
M. CCCCC.
.xx.

[On the back of the leaf is the printer's device.]

---

[1] *Printed* susperiis.   [2] *Printed* petisti.   [3] *Printed* cades.
[4] *Printed* dextriri.   [5] *The contraction for* "pro," *not* "per," *is here used.*

NOTES TO "JOSEPH OF ARAMATHIE."

1. JOSEPH of Arimathea, having been imprisoned by his countrymen for 42 years, is released by Vespasian. On his release, Vespasian asks him how long he thinks he has been in prison. He says he thinks it must be scarcely three days, for he was imprisoned on Friday, and *now it is Sunday*. Thus we may imagine the first extant line to form a part of some such sentence as this—

> "I passed to þis put · and to prisoun eode
> On Frydaye, *sire*," he seis · "*and sonenday is noure*."

The corresponding passage of the French romance may be found at p. 32, vol. i. of the Seynt Graal, ed. Furnivall. "Et vaspasiiens li dist: 'ioseph combien quidies vous auoir este en cheste prison.' Et ioseph li dist, '*Sire*, ie i quit auoir demoure des nenredi iusch'a hui, et ie quit *qu'il soit hui diemenches*. Et nenredi despendi iou le urai prophete de la crois pour qui ie fui en prison mis.' Et quant il eut clie dit, *si commenchierent a rire tout chil qui estoient entour lui*." The last sentence corresponds to our l. 2. The French prose romance is fuller than the present poem, and contains more details. The English poet has evidently aimed at compression, but does not always escape being obscure. The object of these notes is to explain some of these obscurities, and at the same time to point out the signification of some of the *phrases* used. For difficult *words*, recourse should be had to the Glossary. I quote Mr Furnivall's book frequently, referring to it merely by the letters *S. G.*; and I refer to the pages of the *first* volume, unless the second is expressly mentioned. This volume contains the romance in French prose, which, after l. 402 of our poem, is accompanied by the Old English translation made by Henry Lonelich in the time of Henry VI.

7. Joseph was baptized by S. Philip the apostle (S. G. 36), and Vespasian by Joseph.

12—20. This piece is not in the French; nor is it clear whence it is derived.

12. *His fader*. This means that Vespasian fetched his own father and a company of soldiers, and then returned to Jerusalem. History

makes Vespasian's father a man of mean condition, but not so the legend. Vespasian's father was the real emperor at this time, and Vespasian himself only a general. "Et quant vous fustes enprisounes, tyberius cesar estoit empereres de rome, et puis en i a eu trois. Ore est mes peres li quars;" S. G. 32. "When you were imprisoned," says Vespasian to Joseph, "Tiberius was emperor, and since him there have been three [Caligula, Claudius, Nero, Galba, Otho, Vitellius, *six*] and my father is the fourth." Probably "Vespasian and his father" of the legend are, respectively, the Titus and Vespasian of history.

13. An obscure passage. I take *þer þei bosked hem out* to mean "where they came out," where *þei* refers to the Jews who had taken part in the crucifixion. That is, Vespasian and his father returned to Jerusalem, where the Jews who had hidden themselves came out of their hiding-places, and made them to leap down into the pit where they had formerly imprisoned Joseph. This downward leap was one of fifty feet, and the Jews were made to seek for the bottom of it, though they could not see it. Thus they led their life, and remained long there, so that his game (*leyk*) pleased them but little, as long as he remained there. Many other Jews fled for fear out of their own country into the land of Agrippa, Herod's heir, where many exiles were living, deprived of their own land (*or*, forsaken of their own people).

21. *A vois*, viz. the voice of Jesus Christ (see l. 38), who appeared to Joseph in a vision, and told him to leave Jerusalem for ever, and preach the Gospel in other lands, taking with him no provision for the journey except only the Holy Grayl. This accounts for the complaints of Joseph's company; l. 30.

36. *Argos*. "A tant laissa ioseph a parler, si alerent tant ke il vinrent a .j. petit bos, qui estoit a demi lieue de bethanie [l. 29], si auoit nom li bos des *agais*. Et si estoit apieles par chel non, pour chou que en che bos fu agaities herodes thetrarches quant li iuis le liurerent a rethe le roi de damas pour sa fille ke il auoit laissie, quant il prist la seme philippe son frere;" S. G. p. 38. Thus it appears that the wood was called *Agais* (not *Argos*), because Herod the tetrarch was surprised there when the Jews delivered him up to Rethe, king of Damascus, whose daughter he had put away in order to take his brother Philip's wife. Mr Furnivall translates it "the wood of *ambush*," and so Roquefort explains the Old French *agait* by "subtilité, surprise, artifice, piége, *embúche*;" but the verb *agaiter* is explained "examiner avec attention pour surprendre, tendre des piéges," &c.; from which I gather that, though Herod lay hid there, he was caught and taken away. In fact, the Old French verb *agaiter* is identical with the English *await* in form, and with *watch* in derivation and signification. The notion of a wood near Bethany bearing a name which can only be explained in French is precisely what one expects in an old romance. The English poet has even improved upon it; for, finding mention of the king of Damascus, he boldly transfers his *Argos* (though close to Bethany) to the country of Damascus at once.

39. "Et anchois que tu isses de cest bos, feras a m'escuele que tu as vne

petite arche de fust en quoi tu le porteras," &c., S. G. p. 38. i. e. "you
are to make for the dish which you have with you a little wooden box to
carry it about in." The English poet does not explain what " þat ilke
blod" is. It means the blood which was preserved inside the Holy
Grail. The French also tells us that Joseph was to say some prayers
daily on his knees before the box or ark which held the Grail; also, that
Joseph's company were miraculously fed in the wood, and arrived at Sarras
in eleven days.

48. Evidently copied from Exod. iv. 10.

54. *faste bi-syde*, close beside; a common expression; cf. ll. 457, 522.

55. The French romance says the Saracens were named from Sarrás,
but *not* from Sarah, the wife of Abraham, as that would be an absurd supposition; S. G. p. 39. Mediæval etymology (and a great deal too much
modern etymology) is made to depend upon mere *sound*, without reference
to *sense*. The following seems a rational account. "*Saracens*, a name
improperly given by the Christian authors of the middle ages to the Mo-
hammedans who invaded France and settled in Sicily. Concerning the
etymology of this word there have been various opinions. Du Cange
(Glossarium, *v.* Saraceni) derives it from 'Sarah,' the wife of Abraham;
Hottinger (Bib. Or.) from the Arabic word *saraca*, which means ' to steal,
to plunder.' Forster, in his 'Journey from Bengal to England,' derives
it from *sahra*, ' a desert.' But the true derivation of the word is *shar-
keyn*, which means in Arabic ' the Eastern people '—first corrupted into
Saraceni (Σαρακηνοί) by the Greek, and thence into *Saraceni* by the
Latin writers. . . . The name Saraceni occurs in Pliny (vi. 28), and it
seems that it began to be used about the first century of our era, and was
applied to the Bedouin Arabs who inhabited the countries between the
Euphrates and the Tigris, and separated the Roman possessions in Asia
from the dominions of the Parthian kings, &c." *English Cyclopædia;
Arts and Sciences*, vii. 282.

57. þe *temple*, viz. the temple of the Sun, in which was a seat called
the Seat of Judgment; S. G. 41.

63. "He wished to have counsel from his people, and go to meet the
enemy notwithstanding; and they (his barons) have refused to do it, so
that he is sitting there in a very angry mood."

68. *mi foundeor*, my creator, or my patron; viz. Christ.

73. & ȝe *wol*, if ye wish to. The plural *ye* is used as a mark of
deference.

82. *bi holen*, be called. As the prep. *by* is spelt both *bi* and *be* in
Early English, so here the scribe seems to have written *bi* for *be*.

83. *he*, she; the A.S. *heó*; spelt *heo* in l. 87.

85. *for him*, as regards him.

90. In Mr Cowper's Introduction to his "Apocryphal Gospels," p.
xxxiii, he gives several curious stories about the miracles which happened
at Christ's birth, from the "Sermones Dominicales" of Hugo de Prato,
who died in 1322; the same stories are also found in the Legenda Aurea
of Jacobus a Voragine. They include the following. Three suns ap-

peared in the East, and immediately were formed into one ; a Sibyl at Rome told Augustus Cæsar that his greatness was surpassed by that of a child, who suddenly appeared in the lap of a maiden, within a golden circle which was formed round the sun ; the star in the East appeared to the Magi, and in this star appeared a child with a cross on his forehead : at Rome, a fountain of oil gushed out and flowed into the Tiber, and the Temple of Peace fell down ; at Bethlehem, the ox and the ass, standing near the manger, bowed down to Christ, as foretold in Isaiah i. 3, &c. Cf. Piers the Plowman, B. xviii. 230—239 ; also (for the visit of the three kings) B. xix. 71.

91. "And besyde that, is the place where the sterre felle, that ladde the 3 kynges, Jaspar, Melchior, and Balthazar ; but men of Greece clepen hem thus, Galgalathe, Malgalathe, and Saraphie; and the Jewes clepen in this manere, in Ebrew, Appelius, Amerrius, and Damasus.   Theise 3 kynges offreden to oure Lord, gold, encense, and myrre ; and thei metten to-gedre, thorghe myracle of God ; for thei metten to-gedre in a cytee in Ynde, that men clepen Cassak, that is 53 journeyes fro Beth- eleem, and thei weren at Betheleem the 13 day. And that was the 4 day aftre that thei hadden seyn the sterre, whan thei metten in that cytee, and thus thei weren in 9 dayes fro that cytee at Betheleem, and that was gret myracle."   Maundevile's Voiage, ed. Halliwell, 1866, p. 70.

95. The French says Herod killed 140,000 children ; S. G. p. 46.   Our poet says 4140.

99. The story of the idols in the Egyptian temples falling down at the presence of Christ is from the Gospel of Pseudo-Matthew; see Apocr. Gosp. ed. Cowper, p. 63 ; it occurs also in the Arabic Gospel of the In- fancy ; p. 179.   See also the "Cursor Mundi," quoted in Morris's Speci- mens of Early English, p. 138,

> "Quen sco [she, i. e. Mary] was cummen þat kirck witin,
> Man moght a selcuth se to min,
> Þat al þair idels, in a stund,
> Grovelings fel unto þe grund," &c.

111. This speech is given at great length in the French romance ; S. G. pp. 48—54.

117. castest, contradictest, confutest ; lit. throwest over ; cf. l. 703.

120. hou may þis sitte same, how may this agree together ?

121. "He was (Christ's) Father, and for his Son's sake was so called, who was considered to be His Father spiritually, before he was formed as a man."

127. With this explanation of the Trinity compare the one in P. Plowman, B. xvi. 181—227 ; xvii. 124—249.

141. bote I pertly vndo, except I clearly explain.

145. "His Godhead decreased not, though he lighted low, in such a way as to make him not always of the same might ; honoured may He be !"

149. tei for his teeme.   Tei means tugged, pulled hard, drew ; hence it means, "used his best endeavours for his theme."   Unless for is an

error for *forþ*, and then it means "drew forth his theme." The *theme* is the subject of discussion, Gk. θέμα; cf. P. Plowm. B. iii. 95, v. 61, vi. 23.

152. *bar him in herte*, bare (witness) to him in his heart, i. e. admitted to himself as regarding Joseph. To *beren in herte* is almost as untranslatable a phrase as to *beren in honde*, which occurs in Chaucer, Wif of Bathes Prol. 380, and elsewhere. See "Bear in hand" in Nares' Glossary. In the French, Joseph explains that he went barefoot for the love of Christ.

153. *He hedde I-ben*, He would have been; *hedde he ben*, had he been.

159. *heiȝ in him-self*, incomprehensible in itself. *Of tellest*, tellest of.

161. *seie þe*, tell thee. *Haue to done*, have (something) to do, i. e. am engaged.

164. "When our leisure is greater, our power of listening is better."

165. *aboute fifti*. The French says *seventy-five*; S. G. 56.

177. "He was in three kinds of anxiety, and they were these: 1. about the obstinacy of his barons; 2. about Joseph's attempt to convert him; and 3. how God could spotlessly dwell in a maiden."

181. *þreo*, three; this means three trees or stems, or rather, one tree with three stems or trunks, a common symbol of the Trinity, as in P. Plowm. B. xvi. 22, 23. "Si li auint vne auisions, ke il veoit en mi lieu de sa maison la choke d'un grant arbre. . . De chele choke naissoient .iij. ieton mult grant et mult droit et mult haut, et si estoient tout .iij. d'un grant et d'un gros et d'une maniere;" S. G. p. 58.

185. *signede*, signified. The stem with the dim bark signified Christ.

186. *out-wiþ*, without; a Northern form; see Jamieson's Scottish Dictionary.

187. *to kennen vncouþes*, to inform (him) of the marvels.

188. The chamberlain rises from his bed, but, on seeing the vision, falls down for fear; but Evalak lifts him up, and tells him not to be afraid.

189. *feres* in the MS. may be an error for *beres*, which is alliterated to *bad*. See *feres* in the Glossary.

194. *of þreo maner enkes*, of three kinds of inks or colours. "Si uit en cascun des arbres, letres escrites, les vnes d'or, et les autres d'asur;" S. G. p. 59. Here the French omits the *second* or silver ink, evidently by a mistake.

196. Our poet uses the word *wiht* (wight, person) unadvisedly; no person spoke the words, but they were written on the stems. Or we may, perhaps, take *wiht* in the more unusual sense which it sometimes bears, viz. creature, thing, object; a sense still retained in our *no whit*. On the first stem was written *Chist forme* (this makes or creates); on the second *Chist sauue* (this saves); on the third *Chist purefie* (this purifies). The allusion to the Trinity is sufficiently obvious.

200. While he is looking, the three stems seem to coalesce into one, so that he cannot tell what to think of it; S. G. p. 60.

204. The king has a second vision, in which (according to the French) he sees in the wall of his chamber, which was of wood, a door of marble, so neatly fitted into the wall that the joints could hardly be distinguished; and through this door, whilst still closed, he sees a child enter the room and go out again. This denoted the immaculate Incarnation of Christ.

209. *A vois.* In the French, this voice is heard by all the people in the palace, but the king tells the people it is a clap of thunder.

212. Here, as in the English, the French narrative returns to Joseph, who, in a very long prayer, beseeches for success.

213. *how may þis limpe,* &c.; "how will this turn out with regard to this king, who cannot understand?"

215. *Bote ʒif,* &c.,." Unless I convert him at this time, ere he passes hence, he will never be converted." Observe the *future* sense of *beos he,* which is a Northern form.

219. *for no-skunus þinge,* for a thing of no kind, i. e. on no account. The odd form *no skunus* is for *nos kunus,* a contraction of *nones kunes.* The form *any skynes* for *anys kynes* is also found; see my note to P. Plowm. A. ii. 175.

221. *wustest,* didst protect; the French has *garandis,* didst warrant or protect. The verb *witen* sometimes means to protect; as in Seinte Marherete, ed. Cockayne, p. 2, fol. 38, l. 16; and Havelok, l. 405.

225. "Thou didst promise holy church that wouldst exalt her (the church's) strength."

231. Galahad, Joseph's youngest son, was (according to the French) the *ancestor* of the famous men who so increased the renown of Britain; but our translator seems to think he was all one with Galahad, the son of Lancelot and Elaine.

232. *Auentures,* adventures, marvellous deeds.

234. In the morning Joseph arose, and roused all his company, and they prayed before the Grail-Ark, as was their custom; S. G. p. 66.

235. *hit þester bi-gon,* it began to grow dark. The French says nothing about the darkness, only that there was *vn mout grant escrois,* a very great thunder-clap.

236. "Si sentirent *la terre,* qui trambloit desous aus mult durement." S. G. p. 67. The change of *earth* to *grave* is no doubt due to the exigencies of alliteration.

237. Here our poet mentions how Joseph repaired to the ark, which he should have said sooner; see note to l. 234.

243. *Er,* at first, formerly; in the next line, *bote* means *but afterwards.*

251. *Josaphe,* called *Josephes* in the French to distinguish him from his father. Note this distinction.

253. "I will entrust to thee to-day, in a favourable time, a thing that is considered as the most honoured thing on earth; no one else is joyfully to receive it from me, but, on the contrary, each man who after this receives it, is to receive it from thee."

258. Josaphe (or Josephes) on opening the lid of the ark, sees Christ surrounded by the five angels who bear the instruments of the passion.

262. *Three nails;* " trois claus tons sanglens." This is because *one* nail was supposed to have pierced *both* feet.

" The crowne of thorne, þe spere, and nailys *thro.*"
Political, Rel., and Love Poems, ed. Furnivall, p. 111.

264. *lemede,* gleamed or glittered, when driven into the body. This word is clearly only used to obtain alliteration ; it occurs again in l. 687.

267. *he falles ; he ros;* here *he* refers to Josaphe. *He* bad *him,* Christ bade Josaphe.

269. Here Josaphe is supposed to look into the ark a second time, and he now sees the actual Crucifixion.

273. " Pierced with the spear (which) looses (or sets free) blood and water."

274. " Saw (blood) run from them ; (indeed he saw them) run all with red blood, streaming about." The ellipses are very awkward. *Eornen* is another form of the verb *renne.* The French adds, that this blood is seen dripping into the Grail ; which our poet should have mentioned.

277. Josaphe remains in a trance, till his father rouses him ; then both look in together, and see Jesus as He was at the time of the Entombment.

285. The French mentions at least 13 angels, and is fuller. *Twayles* is the Fr. *touailles,* the modern *towels.*

288. *Wasscheles.* The French has—" si en uit issir .ij. angeles, dont li vns tenoit .i. *orchuel* tout plain di aue. et li antres tenoit .i. *jetoir* en sa main destre ; " S. G. p. 72. *Orchuel* is the Lat. *urceolus,* a little pitcher ; *jetoir* is proved by the context (S. G. p. 73) to be a vessel for sprinkling people with holy water. Thus *wasscheles* signifies vessels for holy water ; but the form *wasschel* looks more like a derivative from *wash* than another spelling of *vessel;* see l. 298.

291. I do not find the *name* " Gabriel " in the French ; only that an angel appeared on whose forehead was written—" ie sui apieles forche del tres haut signour ; " i. e. I am called the Strength of the Most High God. This angel does not carry a " sege " or *seat,* but a green cloth, with the Grail resting upon it ; but further on we find an account of a very rich *kaiere* (chair) on which Josaphe is made to sit, which chair was afterwards preserved in the city of Sarras ; S. G. p. 75.

299. *þat geyn weede,* that excellent garment, or rather, clothing, referring to the *vestimens* (Fr. *uestimens*) of l. 294.

300. " And consecrated him as bishop, with both two (of) his hands, and told him about the vestments, what they signified." In the French, he is arrayed with shoes, to keep his feet from evil paths, an upper garment signifying Chastity, an under-garment signifying Virginity, a head-covering meaning Humility, a green garment meaning Invincible Patience, another white one for Justice, a band on the left arm for Abstinence, a necklet of Obedience, and an upper garment over all, which is

Charity. He also holds the staff of Vengeance-and-Mercy, the former being denoted by the bend at the top, the latter by the spiked end ; a ring on his finger, called the ring of Matrimony, and a horned hat, meaning Confession.

302. The oil with which Josaphe was consecrated was kept in the Grail-ark, and afterwards used at the consecration of all the kings of Britain down to Uther-pendragon ; S. G. p. 75.

306. "I commit to thee souls to keep ; if any, through thy fault, fall from my kingdom, at the Day of Judgment thou shalt be sharply reproved." The word *defaute* is from the French " par *defaute* de toi;" S. G. p. 79.

314. *paleys*, palace. This "palace " was the one which had been assigned to Joseph and his company to lodge in. It bore the name of Spiritual Palace (*li palais esperiteus*), a name which had been given to it by Daniel, who had caused this name to be written upon it in black letters in Hebrew characters. But no one at the time knew what the name meant, nor was the meaning ever suspected till it was rendered evident by the lodging of Joseph and his company in it, when they prayed before the Grail-Ark, and the Holy Ghost descended on them ; S. G. 67. Our English version somewhat alters this, obtaining from the word " spiritual " the statement that evil spirits had once dwelt there, l. 315 ; and changing the name into Adventurous or Marvellous. The word *Auntres* is lit. " adventures," but it is probably an error for *Auntrous* (adventurous), which is spelt *Auntrose* in *William of Palerne*, l. 921.

329. *take*, to catch him ; this reminds us of Mark xii. 13.

335. *forsake*, go back from, recall, deny.

345. Josaphe stands up, and his father sits down, feeling himself beaten.

349. This seems to be—" Thou hast seen to-night (that which) signifies to some (that) thou hast made evident to them in what point He (God) is displeased ; thou shalt be visited with vengeance [lit. shalt have vengeance] verily and soon." *Summe* is, apparently, the dative plural of *sum*, the modern *some*. To "diskeuer" is to make plain, reveal.

355. This idea of suffering from an enemy's invasion is probably imitated from 2 Sam. xxiv. 13.

360. In the French, the clerk becomes dumb and blind, but without his eyes flying out of his head. See a very similar story in Chaucer, Man of Lawes Tale, 573.

371. *to fonge þe trouþe*, to receive the truth (will help you) ; in the French, " se tu rechois la creanche ;" S. G. 87.

372. " And what (says Evalac) do you think will befall this man (the clerk who was blind and dumb) ; is recovery in store for him ? " *Tides him hele* is lit. does recovery of health betide him ? The phrase recurs in l. 617, where it means—" is he successful and well ? " The French has— " Et li rois li redist (*answered*), ' Ore me di, iosephe, de chelui qui a perdu la parole et la veue, se il recouuerra iamais ? " S. G. p. 88. Josaphe re-

plies by telling the king to go to the temple of the idols, and to test their might. So the clerk is taken thither accordingly.

376. *Appolin* in the French.

379. The French mentions "lymage martis," the image of Mars, whence the *Martis* of the English version.

385. "The fiend flew out of his body into the air." In the French, it is not Josaphe himself, but the evil spirit which was in the image of Mars, which, by Josaphe's permission, destroyed the image of Apollo as well as all the other images in the temple. Some of the fiends were supposed to reside in the air (Eph. ii. 2); cf. P. Plowm. B. i. 123.

386. *oþure*, others. In the French, the king turns to the image of Mars, and begins to do sacrifice before it, but is stopped by Josaphe, who tells him that he will die on the spot if he persists.

391. The king here goes on to another question, no more mention being made of the blind and dumb clerk. A similar omission occurs in MS. Addit. 10292, which differs somewhat from the Royal MS. xiv. E. iii, the one partly printed by Mr Furnivall, and from which therefore all my extracts are made.

394. The MS. has *vmbe mong ʒongen*, which certainly seems to prove that there was once a word *vmbe-mong*, compounded of *vmbe*, round about, and *-mong*, amongst (A.S. *on-mang*); but I have not found *vmbe-mong* elsewhere. We cannot suppose it an error for *vmbe mon ʒongen* = must go about, because that would refer to the future, whereas the spirit complains that the two Christians are going about already. The verb *ymb-gan* occurs in A.S., meaning *to go round*, and corresponds to the O. Fries. *umbegunga*, Old-Saxon *umbigangan*, Icel. *umganga*, G. *umgehen*.

396. "Il a .ij. angeles auoec lui qui le conduisent et gardent par tous les lieus ou il va; si tient li vns vne espee toute nue, et li autres vne crois ;" S. G. p. 89.

402. Hereabouts begins the English translation by Henry Lonelich, which is defective at the beginning; I give a few extracts below.

405. *Nagister;* called *Ouagre* in the French, and *Oriable* in Lonelich's translation; S. G. p. 91.

406. *keueres vppon*, advances further.

407. *Alongines;* called *Eualachin* in the French, and *Valachin* by Lonelich.

408. The French says 30,000 knights and 60,000 foot; Lonelich has 20,000 horsemen and 40,000 foot; S. G. p. 91.

410. *þei han*. Our poet is certainly wrong here, or else the scribe should have written *han þei; i. e. if* they have gotten that hold, &c. Eualac raised an army to relieve the siege of this town, and succeeded so far, that Tholomer never took it.

414. *bounen*, to prepare, get ready. Mr Morris suggests that it is equivalent to *bannen*, to assemble, but perhaps the former explanation may stand. The adjective *bowne* (ready) is common, but the verb is somewhat scarce. I give three instances from the Percy Folio MS., ed. Hales and Furnivall.

"He bad buske him & *bowne* him : to goe on his message ; "
Scotish Feilde, l. 113.

"Then they *bowned* them, both more & lesse ; " *Eger & Grine*, l. 1325.

"In ladyes [clothes] will yee mee *bowne* ; " *Kinge Adler*, l. 57.

See the adj. *boun* in l. 461.

416. *Carboye;* called *Carabel* in one French version, and *Tarabiel* in another.   Lonelich has—

> "Anon his sonde he dide to sende
> Ouer al tho into euerich ende,
> To alle tho that of him took ony fe,
> Anon with him that thei scholden be,
> And on the morwe to ben gadering
> Atte castel of *Tarabe* with-owten taryenge,
> That twenty miles from Sarras is,
> And fro Valachim sixtene more ne mis (*sic*),
> Where-as Tholomes atte sege was."

Thus in l. 418, the expression "from thence where they lay " means "from the town of Valachim (Alongines) which the enemy were besieging."

420. *Wostou*, knowest thou ; *wendes*, goest.   A mixture of dialectal forms.   Cf. *const* in the next line.

423. Evalac's father was a cobbler in the town of *Miaus* or *Miaux*, i. e. Meaux.

425. *Ouȝte*, possessed, had dominion over.   The story is, that Augustus, hearing that a Child was to be born who would be his Superior, determined to exact homage from his subject states, and demanded from France a hundred-knights, a hundred knights' daughters (our version merely mentions forty of the latter), and a hundred children under five years of age.   Amongst these were two daughters of Count Sevain, lord of Meaux, with whom Evalac went as page.   The girls died, and Evelac, at the age of twenty, was sent by Tiberius as a present to Felis, Count of Syria.   Evelac quarrelled one day with the earl's son, whom he slew, and thereupon fled to the court of Tholomes, king of Babylon, then at war with Holofernes, whom Evelac conquered.   For this service, he received Holofernes' kingdom.

428. *For þou were*, because thou wast.

431. *souȝtes fro*, wentest away from.

433. *woxen vn-sauȝt*, became unreconciled, i. e. quarrelled.

435. *laftest*, didst remain.

436. The French does not say that Tholomes (who may be different from the Tholomer above) was an old man.

438. *For þou toke*, because thou didst take.

446. The cross was made by fastening two strips of red cloth, each a foot long, crosswise upon the shield.

448. *Vigore*, figure.   In one MS. of Chaucer's Astrolabe, *figure* is spelt *vigour* throughout.   The French has *chest signe*, this sign.   Further on, in a passage corresponding to l. 560, Lonelich has—" And the *vigour* of the cros þere he beheld ; " S. G. p. 150.

450. *þis oþer*, these others, *pl.* It means the enemy. Here follows, in the French and Lonelich, a long description of the castle of Valachin.

452. "Tholomer's men got the upper hand, and bore Evelac's men down, and brought them to the ground; then Evelac's men turned again (fled)." Evelac retreated to a castle named Laoines (*Comes* in Lonelich), and Tholomer pursued him hotly. Meanwhile, however, Evelac's subjects in Valachin sallied out, spoiled Tholomer's tents, and retreated again; this is the sense of ll. 455—457.

459. "Then came one spurring quickly to meet him."

463. *scholde*, must, had better.

465. "Therefore she is desirous that he may know it." The queen, by Joseph's advice, warns Evelac that he is in a dangerous place.

472. Evelac, retreating on Sarras, gets more men together, and, in particular, is reinforced by a party of 500 men (Lonelich says 4000) led by Seraphe, his queen's brother, whom he had formerly treated very badly, though not deserving such hatred.

486. "Seraphe, so thou ill oughtest (to have done); it sore repents me that I often ill-used you; for those of one's own kin will ever be friendly, whatever may happen."

489. *þis opere*, these others; as in l. 450.

491. "That they who acted on his advice should rue no attack, through him."

493. "And think, good men, upon the grief that is our children's; (lit. to our children), and what will befall thereof, if we be confounded."

497. *geten on hem*, approached them. It means, the hosts had now approached each other within a glaive's length. This battle took place before a town called *Orkans* or *Orkaus*.

499. "And thrust down the proude ones."

502. "Bore death in his hand, and distributed it around him. He had an axe on high, with a great handle (belve); he held it hard with ligatures (or pressure?) in his two hands; so he smote them with it, and proved his strength, that little might they get away from him, and take to flight. There were steeds to destroy, conflicts to mingle (in); mighty men meet, and hammer through shields; hard hauberks they burst through, and pierced the breast (of the foe); bright shone upon the shaft the blood of heroes. Those that hover about on horse-back hew through helms," &c. Surely a fine passage.

513. *schindringe of scharpe*, cutting of sharp swords; and afterwards died the death, &c.

516. "Hard shields, cloven apart, fell in quarters; (they) slay horse and man wholly at once."

518. *in þe stour lafte*, remained in the battle. In the French, Evelak's steward nearly succeeds in slaying Tholomer himself.

521. *wel a two*, about two. See l. 549.

522. In the French, Tholomer's men flee, and are pursued by Seraphe and Evalac to a narrow pass, where there was a rock which was named

afterwards the "Rock of Blood" from the great loss of life there in this battle. Evalac left some men there to keep the pass, and a second skirmish afterwards took place there; cf. l. 604

527. Tholomer's brother was named Manarcus (Manaquit in the French); he is sent by Tholomer to attack Seraphe; S. G. p. 140.

530. *ascries*, cries out against, shouts against. The French has " si s'escrie," and Lonelich translates—

"Seraphe gan hem *ascrie* mani folde;" S. G. p. 180.

531. *a gome*, a man. This was Manarcus; see l. 536.

539. "Then they fell, for auger, upon Seraphe's knights."

543. While Seraphe is in his swoon, 200 horsemen ride over him, and he is naturally supposed to be dead.

544. *streiȝte to*, stretched his hand towards.

545. *culles on*, strikes upon. Here *cullen* is used merely for *hitting*, just as the E.E. *slen* (*slay*) means both to strike and to slay.

550. "That he might not (go) to him."

555. Evelac was pierced with three glaives, seized by Tholomer's men, and beaten.

558. *forte fallen him feye*, to fell him dead.

560. *Child*, man, viz. Christ. Evelac looks at the red cross so long that at last the figure of Christ appears upon it. *Stremynge on*, streaming with.

562. The white knight is an angel. Similar stories are not uncommon; cf. 2 Maccabees, x. 29. Santiago visibly aided the Spaniards in as many as thirty-eight different battles; Southey's *Pilgrim to Compostella*, note 5. See also Southey's *Roderick* (canto xxv.), where the king is supposed to be an angel.

567. In the French, the white knight only unhorses Tholomer, and sends him prisoner to the town of Orkans.

575. I here give a specimen of Lonelich's translation.

"On of hem drowgh owt a lite knyf,
And wolde hau be-reved Seraphe his lif,
Forto hau smeten him a-middes the fase
Through the oylettes of his helm in that plase.
But ouercomen so was tho Seraphe
That comfort with him myhte non be;
For he was ouercomen so with his blood
So it was merveille that [he] vppe stood,
For on hors power hadde he non to sitte,
Ne of that stede there onys to flytte;
But for febelte that he inne was
Ouer the hors nekke he bowede in that plas,
That power vp to sitte non hadde he,
So that of his purpos failled his eneme." S. G. p. 156.

588. *note*, make good use of; *newed*, renewed.

589. *Haue her-on*, take hold of this; *vppon my bi-halue*, for my sake.

595. "As fresh as a hawk; (yea) fresher at that time than when they advanced thither, at their first onset."

601. Tholomer's steward, named Narbus, rallies his men, and they attempt to retreat by the pass of the " Rock of Blood ; " but " the folk of the Rock " (i. e. those left by Evalac to guard it) utterly rout them.

616. *bi-leued*, left behind. The queen's name was Sarraquite or Sarracynte.

623. " Give me an assurance of that." The queen then offers to pledge her faith : Joseph replies that she has no faith. She asks him what is his belief, and he repeats the creed. The queen also repeats the creed, and admits that she has secretly been a Christian for a long time.

635. The hermit's name was Salustes or Salustine ; he cured Sarracynte's mother, as related below.

645. *heo*, she ; viz. my mother.

646. " Wilt thou believe on this man ? " Sarracynte thinks her mother refers to the hermit, and replies that she will not believe on one so old and gray, but only on one who is as fair as her own brother. She then sees Christ in a vision.

655. *ar þow henne seche*, ere thou go hence.

657. *blusch*, glance. " A wind and a scent wrapped us around ; " i. e. enclosed us. Lonelich has—

> " Many wondirful swetnesse aforn me fyl [*fell*],
> And the hows so ful there-offen was,
> And therto swich delicasie in that plas ; " S. G. p. 174.

660. *Vsede of Goddes bord*, made use of God's table, i. e. administered to us the sacrament, " si fist denant nous ichel saint sacrement ; " S. G. p. 176.

661. " He brought us a writing, which he entrusted to us to keep joyfully." Our version here omits a very long piece about Sarracynte's mother.

674. Insert *he*, which means Joseph.

679. " He had his one arm cut off, which he carried in his other hand."

687. " It seemed to them that he gleamed as light, all in a blaze."

695. Mordreyns is explained to mean " tardieus en creanche," slow of belief. *A lat mon* = a slow or sluggish man ; lit. a *late* man. The healed knight was named Climachideus (*Clamacides* in Lonelich, *Cleomadas* in our l. 692), which means " gonfanonniers au glorieus " (standard-bearer to the Glorious One) ; S. G. p. 178.

698. *let water hize*, caused (or commanded) water to go quickly (i. e. to fly about quickly). *Let* (caused) is nearly always thus followed by an infinitive, and the only infinitive thus spelt is *hize*, to hie, hasten, come or go in haste. *Hize* has nothing to do with *high*, for the latter is spelt *heize* throughout.

702. *nouþer þei nusten*, lit. not where they knew not, i. e. they knew not whither.

703. *casten*, to confute ; cf. l. 117.

704. For the rest of the story, see " The Lyfe of Joseph of Armathy," here printed ; p. 27. The king of North Wales, named Crwdelx, imprisons Josaphe, but is slain by Mordreins ; cf. S. G vol. ii.

708, 709. "Then they (Josaphe and his company) committed the blood (the Grayl) to two men to keep safely, and they depart from the town, and leave the Grayl behind." Lonelich's version has—

> " Than alle tho gan he with him take
> That owt of Ierusalem weren his make,
> Excepte only persones thanne thre
> That he lefte with the Arche [*Ark*] forto be,
> And that holy disch that was there-inne
> It savely to kepen from more oþer mynne [*greater or less*];
> Which on of hem "Enacore" gonne they calle,
> The tother "Manasses," as tho gan falle;
> The thridde was clepid "Lwcan"
> Thi[l]ke same tyme of every man,
> That Ioseph took [*gave*] the Arch in kepinge
> To his purpos as to a man of best levynge;
> And thus these thre leften there
> To kepen this holy Arch in this manere;
> And alle the tothere gonnen forth to gon,
> Cristes name to sanctefien anon,
> And the peple to ȝeven baptiseng,
> And this was alle here labowreng;" &c.   S. G. p. 200.

As the most interesting part of Evelac's early history breaks off here, I think it very likely that the author of our English version, having told about the baptism of Evelac and Seraphe, and leaving the Holy Grail in safe keeping, purposely broke off here; there being nothing to shew that the copy in the Vernon MS. is incomplete at the end.

NOTES TO "THE LYFE OF JOSEPH OF ARMATHY."

THIS one piece has purposely been printed so as to retain the peculiar punctuation of the original, in order to shew the method then in use. Thus, the full stop in l. 11 after the word "prophecye" is used where we should now use a comma, and so on.

P. 27, l. 7. *thantyquytes*, the antiquities; compare *thonourable* in the next line. The unusual words occurring in this piece are explained in the Glossarial Index to it.

P. 30, l. 6. *wyped my face with a rose;* this is hardly a correct translation. Capgrave has—"elevavit me de terra, *rosaque perfudit me, et extergens faciem meam* osculatus est me, et dixit michi," &c. That is, "Christ sprinkled me with a rose, and, wiping my face, kissed me."

P. 30, l. 34. For the story of the Assumption of the Virgin into heaven, see "King Horn, with fragments of Floriz and Blauncheflur, and of the Assumption of Our Lady," ed. Rev. J. R. Lumby (E. E. T. S.). The apostles were all present at it—

> "Come þe apostles euerychon
> To-gidre, but þei wist nouȝt
> How þei weren to-gidre brouȝt." Ll. 304—306.

See also Mr Lumby's preface, pp. vii, viii.

P. 31, l. 16. In Mr Furnivall's "Seynt Graal," vol. ii. p. 125, the number of persons who crossed the sea upon Joseph's shirt is increased to 150, the number left behind being 260.

P. 31, l. 23. In the same work, vol. i. p. 363 and pp. 377—419, "Solomon's ship" is mentioned and described. It was made by order of Solomon's wife, and contained David's sword. See Sir Thomas Maleore's Morte d'Arthur, reprinted by Southey in 1817; or see the "Globe" edition, book xvii. ch. vi. The word "Medor" in the title of Natianiis (Nasciens) is a corruption of the Latin gen. pl. *Medorum.*

P. 31, l. 32. For the account of Crwdelx, king of North Wales, see "Seynt Graal," vol. ii. p. 187; he was attacked by Mordreins and Nasciens, and slain by Gaanort. Celydomus or Celydoine was the son of Nasciens and Flegentyne, who preached to Label, king of Persia, and afterwards married his daughter; he became king of a part of Britain, defeated the Saxons, and was buried at Camelot; Seynt Graal, ii. 221, 377, &c. Observe that "the kynges doughter of Persye" means "the daughter of the king of Persia." The reader will also further observe that *Labell* was rather the name of *the king himself;* but the name is given to the daughter not here only, but also in the verse "Lyfe;" see p. 42, l. 174.

The "Lyfe of Joseph of Armathy" is simply a translation from Capgrave's "Nova Legenda Angliæ;" see the preface. A similar Latin original is printed also in Johannes Glastoniensis, ed. Hearne, vol. i. p. 48. The title is, in Capgrave, "Sequitur extractio de libro antiquitatis glastoñ. de sancto Ioseph ab armathia accepta de libro quodam per theodosium imperatorem inuento in pretorio pi[la]ti in hierusalem." *Nova Legenda,* fol. clxxxvi *b.* This clearly points to the Apocryphal Gospel of Nicodemus, the prologue of which represents one Ananias as translating the said Gospel in the time of *Theodosius;* see Cowper's Apocryphal Gospels, p. 229. The translation is in general very close. It must be noted, however, that the opening sentence—"Forasmuch as often times," &c.—is not found in Capgrave, but occurs in John of Glastonbury in the form following. "Quoniam dubia sæpe legentem fallunt, certa, dubiis ablatis, atque ex antiquis historiagraphorum dictis probata, de antiquitate Glastoniensis ecclesiæ quædam subinseremus." Then follows, in *both,* the Latin text beginning, "Crucifixo Domino, & completis omnibus quæ de eo fuerant prophetata," &c.

The story follows the Gospel of Nicodemus, beginning near the end of Chap. XI, p. 248 of Cowper's edition, where we read of Joseph's imprisonment, his miraculous escape, how he was found at Arimathea, and how the priests and Levites wrote a letter to him, in consequence of which he rode to Jerusalem and there told Annas and Caiphas how Christ had released him, and commanded him not to go out of his house for forty days. At the words in l. 23, on p. 30—"And this sayd and done, Ihesus vanysshed awaye" (*et hijs dictis disparuit*) Capgrave ceases to follow the account in the Gospel of Nicodemus, and I therefore give the remainder of the story in his words.

"Post hec fidei feruore animatus nobilis ioseph ab armathia beati philippi apostoli disciplinatui se tradidit: atque eius salubri disciplina affluenter refertus, ab ipso cum filio suo iosefe baptizatus est. Postea vero a beato iohanne apostolo dum ipse predicationi efesorum insudaret, beate perpetueque virginis marie paranymphus[1] delegatus est, eiusdemque gloriose virginis assumptioni cum beato philippo ceterisque discipulis interfuit. Atque ea que de domino[2] ac de eius genitrice[3] audierat & viderat constanter[4] per diuersas regiones predicauit. Multosque conuertens & baptizans, tandem quinto decimo post[5] beate virginis assumptionem anno, cum memorato filio suo iosefe quem dominus ihesus prius in ciuitate sarath in episcopum consecrauit,[6] ad sanctum philippum apostolum in

[1] Misprinted "*pararüfus*" in Capgrave, but see Hearne's "Johannes Glastoniensis," vol. l. p. 51; where we find *paranimphus.*
[2] Here Hearne's text inserts *Ihesu Christo.*
[3] Here Hearne inserts *Maria.*
[4] Hearne has *instanter.*
[5] Hearne inserts *supradictæ.*
[6] Hearne has *consecrauerat.*

gallias venit. Dispersis enim post ascensionem domini discipulis per diuersa regna orbis terrarum, vt testatur freculfus[1] libro suo secundo, capitulo quarto, reg[n]um francorum predicandi gratia adiens philippus[2] plures ad fidem christi connertit & baptizauit. Volens igitur beatus[3] apostolus verbum dei dilatari : duodecim ex discipulis suis ad euangelizandum vite[4] verbum in britanniam misit, quibus charissimum amicum suum ioseph predictum, qui sepeliuit dominum, vna cum filio suo iosefe prefecit. Venerunt autem cum eis, vt legitur in libro qui sanctum graal appellatur, sexcenti et amplius tam viri quam femine, qui omnes votum vouerunt quod ab uxoribus propriis abstinerent quousque terram sibi delegatam ingressi fuissent. Quod tamen preuaricati sunt omnes preter centum quinquaginta, qui iubente domino mare super camisiam ipsius iosefes transeuntes in nocte dominice resurrectionis[5] applicuerunt in mane. Aliis autem penitentibus & iosefe[6] pro eis orante, missa est nauis a domino quam rex salamon artificiose suo tempore fabricauerat vsque ad christi tempora duraturam : in qua die eadem ad suos socios peruenerunt cum quodam duce medorum nomine naciano, quem ioseph prius baptizauit[7] in ciuitate saram[8] cum rege eiusdem ciuitatis cui nomen mordraius. Cui dominus postea in visu apparens : manus & pedes perforatos cum latere lanciato ostendit. Cui rex quasi multum compatiens dixit ; 'O domine deus meus, quis tibi talia inferre presumpsit ?' Et dominus ; 'Hec mihi,' inquit, 'fecit perfidus rex nort[h]wallie qui seruum meum ioseph nomen meum in partibus suis predicantem cum sociis suis carceri mancipauit, inhumanitus negans eis victui necessaria. Tu ergo gladio tuo accinctus ad partes illas properare ne[9] differas, vt vindictam facias de tyranno et seruos meos soluas a vinculis.' Rex autem euigilans et de visione[10] exultans in domino, disposita domo sua et regno iter cum exercitu suo arripuit : & deo ducente ad locum perueniens regi prefato mandauit quatinus seruos dei liberos abire permitteret. Ille vero mandato eius nullatenus acquiescens, ei cum indignatione mandauit quatinus absque mora de terra sua exiret. Quo audito, rex mordraius venit contra eum cum suo exercitu & duce naciano supramemorato, qui ipsum in bello iusta vltione peremit. Tunc rex mordraius accedens ad carcerem[11] ioseph cum sociis suis in magno gaudio eduxit, narrans ei visionem ostensam a domino super liberatione eorum. Tunc vniuersi gaudio magno repleti immensas gratiarum actiones domino persoluebant.[12] Post hec[13] ioseph cum filio suo iosefe[14] ac decem aliis sociis peragrantes britanniam, regnante tunc in eadem rege aruirago : anno ab incarnatione domini sexagesimo tertio, fidem christi fiducialiter predicabant. Rex autem barbarus cum sua gente tam noua audiens et inconsueta, nec paternas volens in melius commutare traditiones, predicationi eorum [consentire][15] renuebat. Quia tamen de longe venerant, visa vite eorum modestia, quandam insulam siluis, rubis, atque paludinibus circundatam ab incolis ynswytryn, id est, insula vitrea nuncupatam, in lateribus sue regionis ad habitandum concessit : vnde quidam metricus [sic ait][16]

> Intrat auallouiam duodena caterua virorum,
> Flos armathie ioseph est primus eorum :
> Iosephes ex ioseph genitus patrem comitatur ;
> Hijs alijsque decem ius glastonie propriatur.

[1] Printed text, *fretulfus.*
[2] Printed text, *philosophus* (!) "Philippus .... Gallis predicat Christum," &c.; Freculphus, Chronicorum Libri Duo, Tom. ii. Lib. ii. c. iv. Hearne has *adiens plures,* omitting *philippus.*
[3] Hearne—*Sanctus.*   [4] Hearne—*verbum Dei.*   [5] Hearne—*resurreccionis dominice.*
[6] Hearne inserts *memorato.*   [7] Hearne—*baptizaverat.*   [8] Hearne—*Saraz.*
[9] Hearne—*non.*   [10] Hearne inserts—*sibi ostensa.*
[11] Hearne—*carcerem, in quo rex ille iniqus Ioseph inclusum cum suis sociis detinebat, ipsum cum gaudio magno inde eduxit,* &c.
[12] Here the English ceases to follow the Latin, viz. at p. 32, l. 19.   [13] Hearne inserts *Sanctus.*
[14] Hearne inserts *memorato.*   [15] From Hearne.   [16] From Hearne.

Predicti igitur sancti in eodem deserto conuersantes post pusillum temporis per archangelum gabrielem in visione admoniti sunt ecclesiam in honore sancte dei genitricis & perpetue virginis Marie in loco eis[1] celitus demonstrato construere. Qui diuinis admonitionibus obedientes capellam quandam per circuitum virgis torquatis muros perficientes consummauerunt anno post passionem domini tricesimo primo, ab assumptione vero virginis gloriose[2] quinto decimo, eodem autem[3] anno quo ad sanctum philippum apostolum in gallias venerant & ab eo in britanniam missi sunt, ex deformi quidem scemate sed dei multipliciter adornatam virtute. Et cum hec in hac regione prima fuerit ecclesia, ampliori eam dignitate [Dei filius][4] insigniuit, ipsum in honore sue matris principaliter dedicando. Duodecim igitur sancti predicti[5] in eodem loco deo et beate virgini deuota exhibentes obsequia, vigiliis, ieiuniis, & orationibus vacantes, eiusdem virginis dei genitricis auxilio in necessitatibus suis refocillabantur. Quorum comperta vite sanctimonia, alij duo reges, licet pagani, marius aruiragi regis filius et coillus marij filius, vnicuique eorum vnam hidam terre concesserunt ac pariter confirmauerunt, vnde & adhuc duodecim hide per eos nomen sortiuntur. Effluentibus namque paucis annorum curriculis sancti memorati carnis ergastulo sunt educti; inter quos et ioseph sepultus est et positus in linea bifurcata iuxta oratorium predictum. Cepit igitur idem locus esse ferarum latibulum, qui prius fuerat habitatio sanctorum; donec placuit beate virgini suum oratorium redire ad memoriam fidelium.

¶ Hec scriptura reperitur in gestis[6] regis arturi. Ioseph ab armathia nobilem decurionem cum filio suo iosephes dicto & alijs pluribus in maiorem britanniam, que nunc anglia dicta est, venisse & ibidem vitam finiuisse testatur liber de gestis incliti regis arturi; in inquisitione scilicet[7] cuiusdam militis illustris dicti lancelot de lac facta per socios rotunde tabule, videlicet vbi quidam heremita exponit Walwano misterium cuiusdam fontis saporem & colorem crebro mutantis; [8][ubi & scribebatur, quod miraculum illud non terminaretur, donec veniret magnus leo, qui & collum magnis vinculis haberet constrictum. Item in sequentibus, in inquisicione vasis, quod ibi vocant *Sanctum Graal*, refertur fere in principio, ubi albus miles exponit Galnat, filio Lancelot, misterium cujusdam mirabilis scuti, quod eidem deferendum commisit, quod nemo alius, sine gravi dispendio, ne una quidem die poterat portare.]

Hec scriptura inuenitur in libro melkini, qui fuit ante merlinum.

Insula auallonis auida [9][funere paganorum, præ ceteris in orbe ad sepulturam eorum omnium sperulis prophecie vaticinantibus decorata, & in futurum ornata erit altissimum laudantibus. Abbadare, potens in Saphat,[10] paganorum nobilissimus, cum centum [et] quatuor milibus dormicionem ibi accepit.] Inter quos ioseph de marmore, ab armathia nomine, cepit somnum perpetuum. Et iacet in linea bifurcata iuxta meridianum angulum oratorii, cratibus preparatis, super potentem adorandam virginem, [supradictis][11] sperulatis locum habitantibus tredecim. Habet enim secum ioseph in sarcophago duo fassula alba & argentea, cruore prophete ihesu & sudore perimpleta. Cum reperietur eius sarcofagum, integrum illibatum in futuris videbitur, & erit apertum toti orbi terrarum. Ex tunc nec aqua, nec ros celi insulam nobilis-

[1] So in Hearne; Capgrave has *eius*.   [2] Hearne inserts *ut dictum est*.   [3] Hearne—*scilicet*.
[4] From Hearne.   [5] Hearne has—*itaque Sancti, sæpius memorati*.
[6] Hearne inserts *incliti*.   [7] So in Hearne. Capgrave has *inquisitiones*, omitting *scilicet*.
[8] Omitted by Capgrave; supplied from John of Glastonbury.
[9] Capgrave has "funeris, &c.," omitting a passage, which is here supplied from John of Glastonbury, and may be found also in MS. Cotton, Titus D. vii. fol. 29 b; and again, in MS. Arundel 220, fol. 271.   [10] *Marphant* in Cotton and Arundel MSS.   [11] From Hearne.

simam habitantibus poterit deficere. Per multum tempus ante diem iudicia-
lem in iosaphat erunt aperta hec, & viuentibus declarata. Hucusque melkinus."

IIere Capgrave's account ceases, but we find in John of Glastonbury
some verses and a couple of genealogies shewing King Arthur's descent
from Joseph, which I here subjoin.

" *Versus de Sancto Joseph de aurora, quœ & biblia versificata dicitur.*

    Cum sero fieret Joseph decurio dives,
      Civis de Ramatha justus honestus adest.
    Clam servus Christi fuit hic ; a præside corpus
      Postulat ergo Ihesu, præcipit ille dari.
    Præbet opem Nichodemus ei, qui tempore noctis
      Venerat ad Ihesum, corde fatendo fidem.
    Hii mundum corpus involvunt sindone munda,
      Inque petra tumulant, qui petra nostra fuit.

Hæc scriptura testatur, quod rex Arthurus de stirpe Joseph descendit.

Helaius, nepos Joseph, genuit Iosue. Iosue genuit Aminadab. Aminadab
genuit Castellors. Castellors genuit Manael. Manael genuit Lambord & Ur-
lard. Lambord genuit filium, qui genuit Ygernam, de qua rex Uterpeudragun
genuit nobilem & famosum regem Arthurum ; per quod patet, quod rex
Arthurus de stirpe Joseph descendit.

Item de eodem.

Petrus, consanguineus Joseph ab Armathia, Rex Organiœ, genuit Erlan.
Erlan genuit Melianum. Melianus genuit Arguth. Arguth genuit Edor. Edor
genuit Loth, qui duxit in uxorem sororem regis Arthuri, de qua genuit quatuor
filios, scilicet Walwanum, Agraneyns, Gwerehes & Geheries."

Besides the passage just quoted from the "book of Melkin," the
Cotton and Arundel MSS. have a passage, which I here add for the sake
of completeness. It stands exactly the same in both, except that some
of the contractions used are different.

" Ex quo apostoli divisi erant in diuersas regiones predicare verbum dei,
sanctus philippus apostolus sortitus est regionem francie cum suis discipulis.
De quibus misit in britanniam .xij. quorum primus erat Ioseph ab aramathia,
qui et dominum sepeliuit, Anno ab incarnacione domini lxiij. et ab assumpcione
beate marie xv. ; quibus xij. hide a paganis regibus ibidem inuentis erant con-
cesse et confirmate ; qui ibidem commorantes, per gabrielis archangeli admoni-
cionem ecclesiam in honore sancte marie ex virgis torquatis muros perficientes
construxerunt, anno post passionem domini xxxj. ; quam ecclesiam dominus
noster ihesus christus in honore sue matris presencialiter dedecauit, et idem
Ioseph ab aramathia cum filio suo Iosepho et ceteris suis socijs ibidem vitam
suam finisse multi testantur, etc."

A very similar account is given in the Historia Johannis Glastoniensis, ed. Hearne, vol. i. p. 1.

" Anno post passionem Domini trecesimo primo duodecim ex discipulis Sancti
Philippi apostoli, ex quibus Joseph ab Arimathia primus erat, in terram istam
venerunt, qui regi Arvirago renuenti Christianitatem optulerunt. Tamen locum
istum cum duodecim hidis terræ ab eo impetraverunt, in quo virgis torquatis
muros perficientes, primam hujus regni construxerunt ecclesiam, quam Christus
in honorem suœ matris, & locum ad sepulturam servorum suorum præsencialiter

dedicavit. Isti duodecim & eorum successores, diu sub eodem numero heremiticam vitam hic ducentes, magnam multitudinem paganorum ad fidem Christi converterunt."

NOTES TO "DE SANCTO JOSEPH AB ARIMATHIA."

This extract from "The Kalendre of the New Legende of Englande" is a mere epitome of the account in Capgrave's Nova Legenda Angliæ, but all reference to the "book called the Graal" seems to be carefully avoided.

P. 34, l. 3. The Latin hexameters commencing "Intrat Aualloniam" have been already printed on p. 69, in their due place in Capgrave's account.

P. 34, l. 8. The *two kings* were Arviragus and Coillus, as in Cap-'grave's account, on p. 70.

P. 34, l. 10. *whiche to this day be called the .xii. hydes.* . This statement is, I suppose, still true even at the present day. At any rate the mention of " a district, denominated *to this day* 'the twelve hides of Glaston'" occurs in Dugdale's Monasticon, v. i, p. 1; see the whole passage, as quoted in the preface.

NOTES TO THE VERSE "LYFE" PRINTED BY PYNSON, A.D. 1520.

The first 216 lines agree with the accounts already given, and seem to be from the same source, viz. Capgrave's Nova Legenda Angliæ. The latter part of the poem is sufficiently original, and was probably written in the year 1502, or soon after.

L. 5. *v. welles.* i. e. the five wounds. For the story of Longinus, see Piers the Plowman, B. xviii. 78—91, &c. It is taken from the Apocryphal Gospel of Nicodemus.

13. *perysshed,* pierced ; as at p. 31, l. 28. This curious spelling also occurs in some MSS. of Piers the Plowman ; see the footnote to Text B. xvii. 189.

32. The *two cruets* are shewn in the woodcut on the title page ; p. 35.

125. *of ioye seperate;* this corresponds to p. 31, l. 13.

174. See note to p. 31, l. 32.

194. Arviragus, the younger son of Cymbeline, is Shakespeare's Arviragus. See Laȝamon's Brut, v. i. p. 392, and Spenser's Faerie Queene, bk. ii. c. x. st. 52, 53.

234. The 18th year of Henry the Seventh began Aug. 22. 1502, and ended Aug. 21, 1503. The writer is here referring to the numerous cures said to have taken place chiefly in April, 1502 (cf. note to l. 289), but the first cure which he mentions must have taken place in 1501, when two young women of Dolting or Doulting parish, near Shepton Mallet, "made their offering" on St Simon's day, Oct. 28. After this happened many. a miracle (l. 241),-followed by a "continuance of grace" (l. 257), and then the numerous miracles in April, 1502, in the middle of Henry's eighteenth year.

245. *Four hundred* should surely be *fourteen hundred*. If Joseph died in the latter half of the first century (cf. l. 136), this would come nearly right.

258. Banwell lies a few miles to the N.W. of Axbridge.

277. This is the 9th of April, 1502, a Saturday.

282. *lyghtes carè*, Query, Light's Cary, as implied. by the rime. There is also a Castle Cary in the same county.

289. The 10th day of April fell on Sunday in 1502, and as this year was the 18th of Henry the Seventh, it is doubtless this year meant. In fact, this point admits of exact proof ; for, owing to the year 1508 being a leap-year, the 10th of April did not again fall on Sunday till 1513, when "Henry our kyng," mentioned in l. 234, had ceased to exist.

295. St Mark's day ; i. e. April 25, 1502, being Monday.

305. Milborne Port is near the border of Somersetshire, towards Dorsetshire.

313. There are several villages named Compton in Somersetshire, as Compton Bishop, near Axbridge ; Compton Martin, several miles to the Eastward of Axbridge ; Compton Dando, not very far from Bath ; and Compton Dundon, to the S. of Glastonbury. Probably the last of these is here intended.

321. Pilton is on the road between Glastonbury and Shepton Mallet.

370. The story about St David is to the effect that the Saint came to Glastonbury to consecrate the church which had just been rebuilt there, when Our Saviour appeared to him and told him that it had already been consecrated by Himself ; in sign whereof, He caused two holes to appear in the Saint's hands, which closed up again after mass had been said. See Hearne's edition of Johannes Glastoniensis, p. 2.

378. The miraculous walnut-tree is noticed by Camden ; see Chambers' Book of Days, vol. ii. p. 759, and Hearne's History and Antiquities of Glastonbury. St Barnabas' day, June 11, was, before the change of style, the day of the summer solstice ; possibly the budding of the tree was supposed to be influenced by the sun's position in the zodiac.

385. The story of the hawthorn-tree is also quoted by Chambers from Hearne. *Werrall* is a local abbreviation of *Weary-all-Hill*, on the south ridge of which the tree grew. The following account is too good to be passed over. "Concerning the alleged flowering of the tree on Christmas-day especially, there is a curious entry in the Gentleman's Magazine for January, 1753, when the public were under some embar-

rassment as to dates, owing to the change from the old style to the new.—'Glastonbury.—A vast concourse of people attended the noted thorn on Christmas-day, new style ; but, to their great disappointment, there was no appearance of its blowing, which made them watch it narrowly the 5th of January, the Christmas-day, old style, when it blowed as usual.' Whether or not we credit the fact, that the tree *did* blossom precisely on the day in question, it is worthy of note that although the second trunk of the famous legendary tree had been cut down and removed a century before, some one particular tree was still regarded as the wonderful shrub in question, the perennial miracle." Chambers, *Book of Days*, ii. 759.   And this miracle happened less than a hundred and twenty years ago !

401. A PRAYSYNG TO JOSEPH.   Every stanza ends with a similar line, forming a sort of burden.   If the third and fourth stanzas be transposed, these final lines agree better together.   The evident object of the prayer is expressed in l. 452.

P. 52. The office is printed as in Pynson ; but it ought rather to be arranged in lines as under.

Joseph, serue dei
    omnipotentis
miserere mei
    malefactoris.
Esto michi solamen
    in suspirtis,
continuum iuamen
    in molestiis.
Super id quod opto
    da remedium,
& tollatur eo
    quicquid dissonum.

[Sancte ?] Joseph,
    [Christi ?] discipule,
da in futuris
    agenda facere,
in non agendis
    vim hec resistere,
in virtuosis
    vitam terminare,
demum in celis
    tccum habitare.

Versus.   Sancte Ioseph, Christi discipule, &c.
Responsorium.   Intercede pro nobis ad Iesum qui elegit te.   *Oremus.* Domine Iesu Christe, cui omnis lingua confitetur, respice in nos seruos tuos, et placare precibus tui dilecti discipuli Ioseph ; vt, ipso intercedente, mereamur in presentia habere peccati remedium, et in futuro tue visionis dulcedinem.   Qui vivis, &c.

Responsorium.   Serue dei, Ioseph sanctissime,
    preces nostras clementer accipe,
    morbos, cædes, et pestes remoue.
    Et si meremur iam penas luere,
    Christum regem superne glorie
    non iratum, sed blandum effice.

Versus.   Vt cum ceperit mundum discernere,
    et in dextris oues reponere,
    non ira[tum, sed blandum effice]

Oratio.   Omnipotens, sempiterne Deus, &c.

GLOSSARIAL INDEX TO "JOSEPH OF ARAMATHIE."

ABBREVIATIONS, &c.

Dan. Danish.—Du. Dutch.—F. French.—G. German.—Icel. Icelandic.—Lat.
Latin.—A.S. Anglo-Saxon.—Ch. Chaucer.—P. Pl. Piers Plowman.—All. P.
Alliterative Poems (ed. Morris, E.E.T.S.).—Prompt. Parv. Promptorium Parvulorum (ed. Way, Camden Soc.).—Will. of P. William of Palerne (ed. Skeat,
E.E.T.S.), *to which the reader is particularly referred.*
The following are used in a special sense—*v,* a verb in the infinitive mood ; *pr. s.*
present tense, 3rd person singular ; *pr. pl.* present tense, 3rd person plural ; *pt.
s.* past tense, 3rd person singular ; *pt. pl.* past tense, 3rd person plural. Other
persons are denoted by 1 *p.* and 2 *p.* Also *imp.* is used for the imperative mood,
2nd person, and *pp.* for the past participle.

A, *in phr.* wel a two hundred =
about two hundred, 521 ; see also
l. 549.

A-bak, *adv.* backwards, 496. A.S.
on-bæc.

A-bascht, *pp.* abashed, terrified,
202. O.Fr. *esbahir.* See Pr. Parv.
and Partenay.

A-brod, *adv.* abroad, 501.

A-byden him, *vb. refl.* remain,
701.

A-doun, *adv.* down, 642. A.S.
of-dúne. Havelok.

A-dred, *pp.* afraid, 47. Hav.

A-ferd, *pp.* afraid, 203, 412.
Crede. *See* Ferd.

Afurst, *adj.* athirst, very thirsty,
553. P. Pl.

A-grisen, *pr. pl.* grow terrified,
236. Will. of Pal.

Allynge, *adv.* completely, absolutely ; hence, allynge to carpe =
altogether (the right thing) to
speak, quite (the thing) to speak,
440. A.S. *eallunga, eallinga, al-
lunga,* entirely, absolutely, altogether.

Also, as ; also wel = as well,
113 ; also fresch as = as fresh as,
595.

A-mende, *v.* to mend, repair
(shoes), 423.

A-middes, *prep.* amidst, in the
middle of, 602. Ch.

A-morwe, on the morrow, 34 ; *cf.*
" In þe morwe," 26.

An heiȝ, on high, 2 ;—vppon
heiȝ, 503 ;—on heiȝ, 182.

And, if, 48, 389 ; *written* &, 73 ;
and we be = if we should be,
494.

A-non, *adv.* anon, 628, 670. A.S. *on án*, in one; hence, immediately.

A-noþur (*put for* an oþur), a second, 179; another, 378.

An-oygnten, *v.* to anoint, 304. Miswritten *an-oygten* in the MS.

A-pertliche, *adv.* evidently, plainly, 276. Ch.

Ar, *conj.* ere, before, 122, 127.

Armure, *sb.* armour, 563.

A-scries, *pr. s.* cries out to, shouts to, 530. Cf. Sw. *anskri*, an outcry, scream, cry; O.Fr. *escrier*, to call out. Will. of Pal. and Ch.

A-semblet, *pp.* met in a hostile manner, encountered, 520. Will. of Pal.

Asur, *sb.* azure, blue, 194.

Atenes, *adv.* at once, 51; —at enes, 181. Cf. Enes.

Atte, at the, 281, 705. Will. of P.

A-two, *adv.* asunder, in twain, 103.

A-twynne, *adv.* apart, asunder, in twain, 49. Ch.

Auentures, *sb. pl.* adventures, 232.

Auntres, *properly sb. pl.* adventures; *but probably miswritten for* nuntrous, *adj.* adventurous, 320. Cf. *auntrose* in Will. of P.

Auter, *sb.* an altar, 295.

Auȝte, *pt. s.* possessed, 434. *See* Ouȝte.

Ay, *adv.* ever; ay forth = ever after, 126.

A-ȝein, *adv.* again (with the idea of recurrence), 12, 25; back again, 207; in return, 393.

A-ȝein, *prep.* against, 106; him a-ȝeynes, to meet him, in the opposite direction to himself, 459; — a-ȝeines, 562. Will. of P.

Bad, *pt. s.* begged, prayed, intreated, 637, 648. A.S. *biddan*, to ask.

Bad, *pt. s.* bade. *See* Beode.

Bale, *sb.* death, destruction, 502. A.S. *bealu.*

Bar, *pt. s.* bare, 152; —baar, 566; —beer, 502; *pl.* beeren, 453.

Baronage, *sb.* nobility, nobles, 62. Havelok.

Basin, *sb.* 697; —basyn, 286.

Batayle, *sb.* a battalion, squadron, 527, 538; battle, 571.

Bed, *pt. s.* dealt (lit. offered), 502. *See* Beode.

Beden, *pp.* appointed, lit. bidden, 416. *See* Beode.

Beer, *pt. s.* bare, 502; *pl.* beeren, 453. *See* Bar.

Be-hynde, *adv.* in the rear, 30.

Be-knowen, *v.* to confess, 665. [Unless it is two words, *be knowen* = be known.]

Ben, *v.* to be, 248; —beo, 323, 388; —bi, 82; 2 *p. s. pr.* (*with fut. sense*) beost, shalt be, 308; *pr. s.* (*with fut. sense*) beos, will be. 216; 2 *p. pl. pr.* ben, 66; *pr. pl.* beon, 168; —ben, 140; —beþ, 409; —broþ. 331; —aren, 672; *pr. s. subj.* beo, 388; —be, 469; *imp. s.* beo þou, 80; *pl.* beo ȝe, 245; *pp.* I-ben, 153; —I-beo, 469; —be, 626; — ben, 153; 2 *p. s. pl.* were, 428; — weore, 430; *pt. s. subj.* weore, 447; &c.

Bente, *sb.* grassy plain, plain, 450, 489. G. *binse*, a rush.

Beo, *prep.* by, 366.

Beo, Beos, Beost. *See* Ben.

Beode, *v.* to offer, 387; *pr. s.* biddes, bids, 22; *pt. s.* bad, bade, 31, 84, 637, 643; —bed, offered, dealt, 502; *pp.* beden, appointed, 416. A.S. *beodan*, to bid, offer.

Bernes, *sb. pl.* men, 414. *See* Burnes.

Bert, *sb.* beard, 648.

Bi, *prep.* concerning, with regard to. 169.

Bi, *v.* be, 82. See note. Cf. Ben.

Bi-com, *pt. s.* had got to, had taken himself off, 607. So we hear people say, "one wonders *where he is gone to.*" Cf. P. Plow. B. v. 651. Cf. G. *beikommen*, to reach to.

Biddes, *pr. s.* bids, 22. *See* Beode.

Bi-falle, *v.* to befall, 488.

Bi-foren, *adv.* before, in front, 28; before (in point of time), 85, 118; *prep.* in front of, before, 167.

Biggore, *adj. pl. comp.* stronger, 452.

Bigly, *adv.* stoutly, boldly, 571. All. P.

Bi-gonnen, *pt. pl.* began, 575. Or it may be the pp.

Bi-halue, *sb.* behalf, 589; vppon my bi-halue = for my sake.

Bi-heete, *v.* to promise, 67;—bihote, 621, 640. Hav.

Bi-heolden, *pt. pl.* beheld, 686.

Bi-leeue, *sb.* belief, 358.

Bi-leued, *pp.* left behind, 616. Will. of P.

Bi-reuen, *v.* to bereave, 356.

Bi-sydes, *adv.* near at hand, hard by, 527.

Bi-take, *v.* to commit to one's care, entrust, 253; to pledge (one's truth), 624; 1 *p. s. pr.* beo-take, 306; *pt. s.* bi-tauȝte, gave (it to), 661; *pt. pl.* bi-tauȝten, 708. Hav.

Bi þat, by that time, 324; by the time that, 473.

Bi-þenkes him, bethinks him, remembers, 237. Will. of P.

Blencheden, *pt. pl.* looked with blinking eyes; blencheden a-boue = opened their eyes and looked up, 586.

Blusch, *sb.* look, glance, 657. All. P.

Bok, *sb.* a book, 642.

Bone, *sb.* command, 268;—boone, prayer, 227. All. P.

Boone, *sb.* boon, prayer, 227. *See* Bone.

Bord, *sb.* a table, viz. the sacramental table, 660.

Boskes, *pr. s.* gets ready, prepares (letters), 414, 472; *pt. pl.* bosked hem out, came out, 13; *pp.* bosked, royally arrayed, 111;—I-bosket, 153;—bosket, arrayed, in order, 527. *See* Buskes.

Bote, *conj.* except, 43, 141; *adv.* only, 338.

Boþem, *sb.* the bottom (of the pit or prison), 15.

Boto, both two, both, 300. A.S. *bútú, bátwá*, both the two, from *bá*, both, *twá*, two. Cf. *boþe two* in l. 697; and P. Pl. A. ii. 36.

Boun, *adj.* prepared, ready, 26, 461. Icel. *buinn*, prepared. All. P.

Bounen, *v.* to make ready, array, 414;—boune, 472. Troy Book, 827.

Bouwes, *pr. s.* bends *or* makes his way, 571;—bowes to, bends over, 387; *pr. pl.* bouwe, incline, bend (their way), 489; *pres. part.* bouwynde, bowing, bending down, 294.

Bradde, *pt. s.* made broad, i. e. spread open, 642.

Braset, *pp.* lit. braced, i. e. tightly held, 380. *See* I-braced.

Breek, *pt. s.* brake, scattered, 501.

Bren, *imp. s.* burn, 103.

Brimme, *sb.* brim, edge, 458. A.S. *brymme*.

Brusede, *pt. s.* bruised, 501.

Burnes, *sb. pl.* men, 501, 708;—buirnes, 29;—bernes, 414. A.S. *beorn*.

Buskes, *pr. s.* repairs, goes, 202 233, 450; comes, 354. All. P. *See* Boskes.

Byden, *pr. pl.* abide, are waiting, 450;—bydes, wait for, 468.

Carke, *pr. pl.* are anxious, 30. A.S. *becarcan*, to take care concerning (Lye); A.S. *carc, cearc*, care; mod. E. *cark :* cf. O.H.G. *karc, karch, charch*, clever (*perhaps originally* solicitous). See *Carking* in Atkinson's Cleveland Glossary. It occurs in the *Plowman's Tale*.

Carpen, *v.* to speak, 175, 615 ;—carpe, 440; 1 *p. pr. pl.* we speak, 212. Will. of P.

Casten, *v.* to confute, refute, 703; 2 *p. s. pr.* castest, 117. Lit. it means to throw, or overthrow; cf. Sw. *kasta*, Dan. *kaste*. See *Kest* in All. P.

Chaumbre-wouh, *sb.* chamber-wall or wooden partition, 204.

Cher, *sb.* countenance, 83.   Ch.

Child, *sb. used of a grown-up person*, viz. Jesus, 560.

Childre, *sb. pl.* children, 493.

Clanses, *pr. s.* cleanses, 198.

Clepeþ, 2 *p. pl. pr.* ye call, name, 379 ;—clepen (*either inf. or pr. pl.*), 692. A.S. *cleopian*.

Clergye, *sb.* learning, 171. P. Pl.

Come, 2 *p. s. pt.* didst come, 434 ; *pt. s.* com, there came, 21; *pl.* comen, 91, 283 ;—come, 35 ; *pp.* comen, 622.

Come, *sb.* coming, method of approach, 206; coming, advance, 596.

Con, *pr. s.* he knows, 171 ; 1 *p. s. pr.* I can, 402; 2 *p.* const, canst, 401, 421.   *See* Cunne.

Coroune, *sb.* crown (viz. of thorns), 263.

Cristendom, *sb.* Christianity, 632, 662.

Cristene, *v.* to Christianize, 703.

Crois, *sb.* a cross, 446.

Cruetes, *sb. pl.* cruets, 287.

Cuiþe, *v.* to make evident, shew, 484. See *Kiþen* in Will. of P.

Culles, *pr. s.* strikes ; culles on = strikes upon, hits a *killing* blow upon, 545.

Cun, *sb.* kin, 422.

Cunne, *pr. s.* 1 *p.* I know, 48 ; —con, 402; *pr. s.* con, 171; 2 *p.* const (canst), 401, 421.

Cuþþe, *sb.* native country, 18; —kuþþe, country, kingdom, 434. A.S. *cýððe*, a region, native country. All. P.

De-deyn, *sb.* disdain, 244. See *Dedain* in Will. of P.

Defaute, *sb.* fault, 307.

Demayȝen, *v.* to fear, be dismayed, 31;—demayen, 84. Span. *desmayar*, to be dispirited. Cf. O.Fr. *esmaier*, to amaze. See *Demaye* in Halliwell.

Deore, *adv.* dearly, 69.

Dere, *adj.* noble, excellent, i. e. fertile, 37. Cf. "þe *dere* kynge," "his *dere* kuyghttes," *Morte Arthure*, 1601, 1602.

Derne, *adj.* secret, 576. Ch.

Derue, *v.* to afflict, harm, 47 ; *pt. s.* deruede, vexed, 535. A.S. *deorfan*, to toil; O.Fries. *forderva*, to perish ; G. *verderben*, act. to spoil, neut. to perish.

Deþ, *sb.* death (with þe prefixed), 514, 534.

Digne, *adj.* worthy, 252. Ch.

Discounfitede (*read* discounfited), *pp.* discomfited, 61.

Diskeueret, *pp.* disclosed, 350. It means that Evelak had disclosed the marvels which he saw to his chamberlain.   Hem = them, sc. the marvels.

Dispit, *sb.* despite, harm, injury, 581. See *Despit*, Will. of P.

Diȝen, *v.* to die, 495 ; dye, 390 ; *pt. s.* diȝede, 132, 134.

Diȝt, *pp.* dressed, prepared, ready, 34. Cf. I-diht. Ch.

Don, *v.* to do, 26 ;—done, *in phr.* haue to done = have to be busy, 161:—do [þe] to preue, cause [thee] to experience, 389 ;—do in, put in, 40; *pr. s.* dos, 233 ; causes, 252 ; *pl.* don hem to ȝonge, set out to go, 34; *pt. s.* dude, 90 ; caused, 129 ; 1 *p. pl. pt.* duden, did, 659 ; *imp. s.* do awei, put away, 102 ; do me, give to me, 623; do tel me, 391 ; *pp.* do, 524.

Dorste, 1 *p. s. pt.* I durst, 664.

Douhtilyche, *adv.* doughtily, bravely, 495.

Douȝti, *adj.* doughty, 480. Will. of P.

Dredde, *pt. s.* dreaded, 132.

Duntes, *sb. pl.* dints, blows, 598. See *Dint,* Will. of P.

Duppes, *pr. s.* dips, dives, drops, 534.

Eft, *adv.* again, 359.

Eir, *sb.* heir, 19.

Eiþer, each (of them), 286.

Eiȝen, *sb. pl.* eyes, 362.

Eke, *adv.* also, 22, 160.

Elles, *adv.* otherwise, in another way, 119, 256.

Enes, *adv.* once, 25 ; at enes = at once, 181, 517.

Enkes, *sb. pl.* inks, colours, 194. Fr. *encre.* See Wycliffite Glossary.

Er, *conj.* ere, before, 524. *See* Ar.

Eodest, *pt. s.* wentest, 4, 641 ; *pt. pl.* eoden, 326.

Eornen, *pr. pl.* they run, flow ; cornen of blod = they drip with blood, 275. A.S. *yrnan,* to run. Cf. Renne.

Er, *adv.* formerly, once, at first, 242. *See* Ar *and* Erest.

Erest, *adv.* erst, first, 56. A.S. *érest,* from *ér. See* Ar.

Est, *sb.* the east, 91.

Euel, *sb.* disease, 644.

Euel, *adj.* hard, difficult, 667.

Falle, *v.* to happen, befall, 190 ; hit falles not = it is not possible, 598. Will. of P.

Fallen, *v. tr.* to fell, 558 ; *pt. s.* fel, struck, 569 ; *pt. pl.* fullen to = felled upon, struck violent blows on, 539.

Fare, *v.* to go, 63 ; fare to hem = go to meet them, i. e. the enemy; —faren, 506 ; *pt. s.* ferde, fared, went, 28, 557 ; *pl.* ferden, 53, 368 ; contrived to do (with little), 626 ; aȝeyn ferden, returned, 558 ; *pt. s.* ferede, should prove to be, 413. A.S. *faran.* Will. of P.

Faste, *adv.* close, 522, 635. So in *Will. of Palerne,* 3.

Fastenen, *v.* to fasten, 249 ; *pp.* fastned, 626.

Faus, *sb. either* (1) haste (the modern *fuss*), *or* (2) falseness, defect, deceit, 208. The alliteration renders it probable that the latter is right, and that it merely repeats *faute* under another form. Roquefort gives *faucer,* to deceive, *faus,* false, and the mod. Fr. *faux* is a *sb.* as well as an adj.

Faute, *sb.* fault, defect (in the wall), 208.

Fayn, *adv.* gladly, 179. Will. of P.

Faynede, *pt. pl.* gladdened, flattered, 243. A.S. *fægenian,* to rejoice.

Feire, *adv.* fairly, suitably, 564.

Fel. *See* Fallen.

Fel, *pt. s.* fell, 582.

Felauschipe, *sb.* intercourse, 84 ; —felauschupe, a company, set of companions, 165.

Felde, *pt. s.* fell, 203. Hence possibly, in l. 2698 of Havelok, we may read ne *felden,* did not *fall,* instead of "did not *fell.*"

Felle, *v.* to fell, 368. Hav.

Feol, *adj.* fell, fierce (?), 665. An unusual spelling.

Feole, *adj. pl.* many, 18, 90, 100, 147.

Feor, *adv.* far, very much, greatly, 552 ; bi fer = by far, 592.

Ferd, *sb.* fear, 188. *See* Fert.

Ferd, *pp.* afraid, 189.

Ferde, *sb.* a host, army, company, 12. A.S. *ferd, fyrd.*

Ferde, Ferden. *See* Fare.

Ferede, *pt. s. subj.* fared, i. e. should turn out to be, 413. *See* Fare.

Feres, prob. an error for *beres* = bears. 189 ; for this seems to suit the alliteration better. Yet *feres* may be from the A.S. *férian,* to convey, carry; whence our *ferry.* See *ferien* in Stratmann.

Ferli, *adv.* wonderfully, 154.

Ferli, *sb.* wonder, marvel, 210. Will. of P.

Ferly, *adj.* wonderful, 568.

Fert, *sb.* fear, 18 ;—ferd, 188.

Fette, *v.* to fetch ; lette fette = caused to be fetched, 167 ; *pt. s.* fette, 12, 147. Ch.

Feye, *adj.* dead, 558 ;—feiȝe, 569 ; *pl.* feye, 368. A.S. *fǽge,* Icel. *feigr.*

Fleih, *pt. s.* flew, fled, 98 ;—fleyȝ, 385 ; *pl.* flowen (fled), 18 ; (flew), 362.

Flote, *sb.* a troop, company, 28. O.Fr. *flote,* a troop ; Low Lat. *flota,* a *fleet* of ships ; from *fluctus.*

Flowen. *See* Fleih.

Fluiȝt, *sb.* flight, 506.

Folewede, *pt. pl.* followed, 28 ; *imp. pl.* fol**eweþ, 245 ; *pres. part.* folewynde, 551 ; *pp.* folewed, 569.

Folfulle, *v.* to fulfil, 68.

Folfulsened, *pp.* fully accom-

plished, 618. From *fol* = full, and *fulsen* = *fulsten,* A.S. *fylstan,* to aid, support, the stem of which agrees with the O.H.G. *follest* or *volleist,* completion; from the root of *full.* It is thus a strengthened form of to *fulfil.*

Folwed, Folewede, Folewen. *See* Fulwed.

Fond, *pt. s.* found, 242, 462.

Fondes, Fondet. *See* Founde.

Fonge, *v.* to apprehend, attain to, 371 ;—fongen, to receive, 622 ; *pr. s.* fonges, takes, 52 ; draws, 568 ; *pt. s.* fongede, took, 143. All. P.

Fontston, *sb.* a font-stone, a font, 7. See Hampole, *Pr. of Consc.* 3311. Ch.

Foorme, *sb.* form, 561.

Foote, *sb. pl.* feet (in measurement), as we now sometimes say " a hundred foot," 14.

For, *conj.* because, 428, 438.

For, *prep.* as regards ; for him = as regards thy child, 85.

Fore, *adv.* forth, 110. Fore telle = tell forth, declare ; cf. Life of Beket, ed. W. H. Black, 31. Fore seiden = said beforehand or declared, 208.

For-fouȝten, *pp.* exhausted with fighting, 577. Will. of P.

For-let, *pp. either* abandoned, forsaken; *so that* for-let of heore oune = forsaken by their own people; *or else* deprived, i. e. of their own land. The latter makes the better sense, but lacks authority. *For-lete* (= forsaken) occurs in Alexander, l. 679 (printed in the appendix to William of Palerne), and in the Wycliffite Glossary.

Forme, *adj.* first, 685. Mœso-Goth. *fruma,* first.

Forsake, *v.* to deny ; *pp.* forsaken, refused, 64. See P. Plowman, B. v. 431.

For-set, *pp.* set aside, snubbed, 487. Cf. A.S. *forsittan*, to neglect.

Forsoþe, *written for* for soþe, i. e. for the truth, in truth, 3, 36, 99; cf. l. 523.

Forte, *put for* for to, 15, 40, 116, 199, 703.

Forþ wiþ, right against, over against, 267.

Forþi, *conj.* on that account, 439, 465. *But in* l. 603 *it seems to mean* on what account, wherefore, why.

Forþinkes, *pr. s. impers.* it repents me, 487. Will. of P.

Forþward, *adv.* forward, 53. Will. of P.

For-ȝiue, 1 *p. s. pr.* I forgive, 250; 2 *p. s. pt.* for-ȝaf, didst forgive, 223.

Founde, *v.* to go towards, approach (*with* dat.), 367;—founden, to go, 506; *pr. s.* fondes, goes, 537; *pt. s.* fondet, came, 12; *pt. pl.* foundeden, went forward, advanced, 596. In a slightly different sense, *pt. s.* fondede, tried, proved, 505. See *Fonden*, Will. of P.

Foundeor, *sb.* founder, Maker, Creator, 68, 673. O.F. *fondeur*, a creator.

Frusschede, *pt. pl.* bruised, dashed in pieces, 505. Fr. *froisser*.

Fuir, *sb.* fire, 260.

Fullen, *pt. s.* fell; fullen to = fell upon, 539. The spelling *fullen* occurs in the Castle of Love, ed. Weymouth.

Fullouȝt, *sb.* baptism, 682;—fullouht, 693. A.S. *fulluht*.

Fulwede, *pt. s.* baptized, 683;—folwed, 691;—folewede, 10;—folwede, 694; *pp.* fulwed, 699; *pr. pl.* folewen, 8. A.S. *fulwian*.

Gete, *v.* to beget, 230; to get, obtain, 23; *pp.* geten, *in phr.* geten on hem = approached towards them, i. e. they were within a glaive's length of them, 497; attained, reached, 523.

Geyn, *adj.* suitable, 299. In N.E. *gain* is near, direct, handy, convenient; O.Swed. *gen*, direct; Icel. *gegn*, direct, ready, from Icel. prep. *gegn*, over against, cf. G. *gegen*, against; Sw. *gen*, near.

Geynliche, *adv.* suitably, conveniently, 298.

Gleyue, *sb.* a glaive, falchion, curved sword. 497. W. *glaif*, a crooked sword.

God, *adj.* good, 66. See Greiþe.

Gome, *sb.* a man, 531. Will. of P.

Gon, *v.* to go, 24, 82; *pr. pl.* gon, 702; *imp. pl.* gos, 373.

Gost, *sb.* spirit, 49, 315. Ch.

Gostliche, *adv.* spiritually, 122, 135; *adj.* spiritual, 280.

Grame, *sb.* anger, vexation, 539. Ch.

Greiþe, *v.* to array, 299. Icel. *greiða*. Will. of P.

Greiþe, *sb.* preparation, arrangement; god greiþe = good arrangement, i. e. satisfactory, 66; hi god greyþe = satisfactorily, admittedly, 341. Icel. *greiði*.

Greiþli, *adj.* excellent, 88. Very rare as an adj.

Gretnede, *pt. s.* became great (with child), 88.

Gultus, *sb. pl.* guilts, sins, 249.

Ha. See Hauc.

Hache, *sb.* axe, 503, 544, 587. Cf. Pol-hache.

Hakken, *pr. pl.* hack, cut, 512.

Halp, 1 *p. s. pt.* helped, 484; *pt. s.* 675.

Halse, 1 *p. s. pr.* I entreat, conjure, 400. Ch.

Halt, *pp.* held, esteemed, 122.

Halue, *sb.* a helve, haft (of an axe), 503. A.S. *helf, hielf.*

Halue, *sb.* side (lit. half), 549. Ch.

Haly, *adj.* holy, 288, 314.

Haspet, *pp.* fastened with a hasp, 205. A.S. *hæpsian.*

Hauberkes, *sb. pl.* hauberks, 509. Ch.

Haunsen, *v.* to enhance, exalt, increase, 225, 232. "Hawncyn, or heynyn, hawtyn, hawnsyn or yn heyyn, hawten or heithyn vp, *Exalto, elevo, sublevo.*" Prompt. Parv. Halliwell quotes *Hanse,* to exalt, from the Coventry Mysteries. The French romance has the word *essauchier* thrice, in this passage; *see* Hiȝen.

Haue, *v.* 63 ;—ha, 351, 578 ;—han, 524 ; 1 *p. s. pr.* haue, 141 ; 2 *p.* hast, 350 ; 3 *p.* has, 405 ; 2 *p. pl.* han, 247 ; 3 *p.* han, 61, 469 ; *pt. s.* hedde, 503 ; *pt. pl.* hedden, 244 ;—hadden, 474 :—haden, 676 ; *imp. s.* haue (þou), 210, 589 ; *pt. s. subj.* hedde, would have, 153.

He, *pron. fem.* she, 83 ;—heo, 87. A.S. *heo.*

Hedde, Hedden. *See* Haue.

Heiȝ, *adj.* high, 153 ; exalted, mysterious, 159 ; — heiȝe, 698 ; *superl.* hiȝeste, 254. Vppon heiȝ, on high, 503.

Heiȝþe, *sb.* height, 192. Cf. *Heȝþe* in All. P.

Hele, *sb.* health, prosperity, success, 617 ; recovery from sickness or disease, 372, 634, 637. All. P.

Helede, *pt. s. intr.* healed, became whole, 681. Will. of P.

Hem, them, 31 ; *dat.* heom, 367.

Henne, *adv.* hence, 215, 641. Ch.

Hente, *pt. s.* caught hold of, seized, 382 ; hente vp, caught up, caught and lifted, 532. Ch.

Heo, (1) she, 87, 461 ; (2) he, 97 ; (3) they, 283 ; *dat. pl.* heom, 130.

Heold, *pt. s.* held, 134, 360, 591 ; heold þider, went thither, 113 ; —huld, 504 ; *pl.* heolden, considered, 430 ; *pp.* holden, considered as, 95, 254 ;—halt, 122 ; *imp. pl.* holdes ou, keep yourselves, 492. *See* Huld.

Heom. *See* Heo *and* Hem.

Heore, their (*lit.* of them), 18, 20, 101 ;—here, 30.

Heowen, *pr. pl.* hew, 511.

Herbarwe, *sb.* harbour, lodging, accommodation, 30 ; — herborwe, 32. Ch.

Here, *v.* to hear, 45 ;—heere, 109 ; *pt. s.* herde, 31 ; *pt. pl.* herden, 2.

Herre, *adj. comp.* higher, 430. A.S. *hyrra.*

Hete, 1 *p. s. pr.* I promise, declare, 412, 669. Ch.

Hetteston (*for* hettest þou), 2 *p. pr. s.* art thou called, 155. Ch.

Heuior, *adj. or adv.* heavier, 592.

Him, *in dative case,* to him, 21.

Hise, *pl. possess. pr.* his, 24

Hit, *neut. pron.* it, 440.

Hiȝe, *v.* to go quickly, *in phr.* he let water hiȝe, he caused water to go about quickly, 698. *Hiȝe* is sometimes used in the sense of "to cause to hasten," as in Will. of P. 1482, and this seems to be the construction here—"he caused water to fly about."

Hiȝen, *v.* to exalt, 226 ; *pt. s.* 2 *p.* heiȝtest, didst exalt, 225. Here the idea of *exaltation* is *thrice* repeated in the words heiȝtest, haunsen, hiȝen. So also in the French —"pour ton non *essauchier* et aleuer . . . . car tu le dois *essauchier* et *acroistre* . . . . ke ele [*l'eglise*] soit *essauchie* et *acreue,*" &c. Seynt Graal, p. 64. *Hiȝen* should rather be spelt *Heiȝen.*

Hiʒtest, *pt. s.* 2 *p.* didst promise, 109. Cf. Hete; see Will. of P.

Ho, *pron. inter.* who, 466, 674.

Holden, *pp.* reckoned, held (to be), 95, 254; *imp. pl.* 2 *p.* holdes on, hold yourselves, keep yourselves, 492. *See* Heold.

Hole, *adj. pl.* whole; þreo hole = whole three, 340;—hol, *sing.* 681. Will. of P.

Holliche, *adv.* wholly, 51, 86, 134, 456.

Holt, *sb.* hold, citadel, 410.

Hom, *sb.* home, 602; hom wende = to go home, 609.

Honden, *sb. pl.* hands, 272;—hondes, 300, 697.

Hondred, hundred, 476.

Honginge, *pres. part.* hanging, 205.

Hor, *adj.* hoar, hoary, 648.

Hors, *sb.* a horse, 563.

Horses, *pr. s.* sets upon a horse, 570.

Hoten, *pp.* called, named, 79, 82, 231;—i-hoten, 291.

Houen, *pr. pl.* halt, hover about, 489, 511. All. P.

Hudden hem, *pt. pl.* hid themselves, 13.

Huirne, *sb.* corner, nook, 378; *pl.* huirnes, corners, nooks, hiding-places, 13. Cf. *Hirne* in Ch.

Huld, *pt. s.* held, 504; *pt. pl.* hulden (hem), defended (themselves), 512, where the context would rather require the present tense. Cf. Heold. A.S. *healdan*: cf. *hálla* in Ihre's Glossary.

Huppe, *v.* to hop, leap, leap down, 14.

Huttes, *pr. s.* hits, 532.

I-ben, *pp.* been, 153;—ben, 153.

I-blesset, *pp.* blessed, 240.

I-boren, *pp.* born, 89;—i-bore, 119;—boren, 163, 430.

I-bosket, *pp.* well arrayed, finely dressed, 153. *See* Boskes.

I-braced, *pp.* tightly fastened, 265. *See* Braset.

I-called, *pp.* called, named, 78, 479;—called, 156.

Icholde, *put for* ich wolde, I would, 67.

Ichul, *put for* ich wol, I will, 253.

I-cloþed, *pp.* clothed, draped, 295.

I-come, *pp.* come, 403.

I-liht, *pp.* arrayed, 476.

I-fet, *pp.* fetched, brought, 428.

I-folwed, *pp.* baptized, 7. *See* Fulwede.

I-graunted, *pp.* granted, 280.

I-helet, *pp.* healed, 650.

I-hoten, *pp.* named, called, 291.

Ilke, *adj.* same, very; þis Ilke, 6, 279, 353; þat Ilke, 40, 282; wiþ þat Ilke, forthwith, 565, 573.

In, *sb.* lodging, 163.

Inne, *v.* to lodge, 166; *pr. s. act.* innes, provides with lodgings, 174.

Inne, *adv.* in, within, 221. Ch.

Ioyned, *pp.* lit. enjoined; hence, reproved, 308. See Halliwell, and cf. *ioyned* = appointed in Allit. Poems, ed. Morris, B. 877.

Ioynes, *pr. s.* approaches (lit. joins), 407.

I-seo, *v.* to see, 498.

I-seʒe, *pp.* seen, 349.

I-slawe, *pp.* slain, 96.

I-strauʒt, *pp.* stretched, 269.

I-swowen, *pp.* thrown into a swoon, 203.

I-tornd, *pp.* converted, 216.

Iugget, *pp.* judged (to be), considered, 251.

I-worpe, *pp.* cast, thrown, 221. See Warpes.

I-writen, *pp.* written, 317.

Kenne, *v.* to make known, teach, 158;—kennen, to inform, 187 (where *him* must be understood); —kennes, *pr. s.* makes known, teaches, 198; instructs, bids, 446; *pp.* kenned, informed, told, 466. Will. of P.

Keuered, *pp.* covered, 176 ; *pt. s.* keuerde, 263.

Keueren, *pr. pl.* achieve ; *hence,* keueren on = achieve their onward way, go forward, 27. See *William of Palerne* and *Gawayne and the Grene Knyʒt.* Similarly, *keueres vppon* = advances, 406.

Kuþþe, *sb.* kingdom, country, 434. See Cuþþhe.

Kuynde, *sb.* nature, 106, 131, 133; *pl.* kuyndes, 136. þe kuynde = those allied by nature, those that are akin by birth, 488.

Lacche, *v.* to catch, get hold of, take prisoner, 356 ; *pt. s.* lauʒte, took, received, 222. Will. of P.

Ladden, *pt. pl.* led, 16. Will. of P.

Laft, *pp. (of trans. vb.)* left, 540. See Leuen.

Laftest, 2 *p. s. pt.* didst remain, 435 ; *pt. s.* lafte, remained, 518 ; *transitive,* lafte, left, 707. Will. of P.

Lai, Leiʒen. See Liggest.

Lat, *adj.* slow (lit. late), 695. Mordreyns is supposed to mean "slow of belief." All. P.

Lauhwhen, *pr. pl.* laugh, 2.

Lauʒte, *pt. s.* took, received, 222. See Lacche.

Lees, *pt. s.* lost, 125. Cf. P. Pl. B. vii. 158.

Leeue, *v.* to believe, 105, 640 ;— leeuen, 219 ;—leue, 646 ; *pt. pl.* leeueden, 101 ; *imp. s.* leeue, 99.

Lemede, *pt. s.* gleamed, glittered, 264;—leomede, 687. Ch. has the *sb.*

Lenden, *v.* to arrive, come, 81 ; *pr. s.* lendes aʒein = arrives back again, i. e. retires, departs, 207 ; *pr. pl.* lenden of, go out of, depart from, 709. Cf. A.S. *lendian,* to land.

Lenes, *pr. s.* lends, gives, imparts, 590 ; *pt. s.* lente me of = imparted to me some of, 5. Ch.

Lenge, *v.* to remain, dwell, stay, 162, 603 ; *pr. s.* lenges, lingers, 207 ; 2 *p.* lengest, lingerest, 277 ; 2 *p. s. pt.* lengedest, 429 ; *pt. pl.* lengede, 16, 17 ; *pres. part.* lenginde, 20 ; *pp.* (wast) lenged, didst dwell, 425. Will. of P.

Lengore, *adv.* longer, 137.

Leodes, *sb. pl.* people, folks, men, 168, 585. See *Lud,* Will. of P.

Leomede. See Lemede.

Leones, *sb. pl.* lions, 222.

Leoue, *adj. pl.* dear, 240.

Leres, *pr. s.* teaches, 305. Will. of P.

Lette, *pt. s.* caused, 94, 167, 173 ; *where* lette fette = caused to be fetched, lette lede = caused to be led ;—let hiʒe (*see* Hiʒe), 698. See *Leten,* Will. of P.

Leue, *v.* to believe, 646. See Leeue.

Leuen, *pr. pl.* leave, 709 ; *pt. s.* lafte, left, 707 ; *pp.* laft, 540.

Leyk, *sb.* play, game, 17. Sw. *lek.*

Leyser, *sb.* leisure, 164. Ch.

Lide, *sb.* lid, 41, 257. A.S. *hlid.*

Liggest, 2 *p. s. pr.* liest, 278 ; *pt. s.* lai, 176 ;—lay, 266 ; *pl.* leiʒen, 418. Ch.

Lihte, *v.* to alight, 81 ; *pr. s.* lihtes, 584 ; *pt. s.* lihte, alighted, 116, 145. A.S. *lihtan.*

Lihten, *pr. pl.* kindle, 191.

Lihtned, *pp.* relieved, 644.

Liked, *pt. s. impers.* it pleased (with *hem* understood); luyte liked his leyk, his game pleased them little, 17. Will. of P.

Limes, *sb. pl.* limbs, 151. Ch.

Limpe, *v.* to happen, turn out, 213; *pr. s. subj.* lympe [MS. *lyme*], may happen, 370. A.S. *limpan:* see *Lympe,* All. P.

Liueraunce, *sb.* free provision, 163. From Low Lat. *liberare,* to give, bestow.

Liuere, *v.* to deliver, 707. Halliwell.

Lokynde, *pres. part.* looking, 278.

Loueliche, *adv.* gladly, 281; kindly, 305. A.S. *lufelíce,* lovingly, willingly, gladly; Bosworth.

Louses, *pr. s.* looses, sets free, causes to flow (with a preceding *þat* understood), 273; *pt. s.* lousede, let go, 599; *imp. s.* louse, loose thou, open, 49.

Lufte, *sb.* air, sky, 385. Laȝamon.

Lust, *pr. s. impers.* it pleases, 41.

Lustnynge, *sb.* listening, attention, 164.

Luttulde, *pt. s.* became small, diminished, lessened, 145.

Luyte, *adv.* little, in a small degree, 17;—luite, 148;—much ne luyte, much nor little, 481.

Luyte, *adj.* little, 554; *pl.* few, 506;—luytel, 39, 644.

Lympe. *See* Limpe.

Lynde, *sb.* the linden or lime tree, 585. A.S. *lind, linde.* Cf. Chaucer, Rom. Rose, 1385; Clerkes Tale, Lenvoye, 35; and F. Plowman, B. i. 154.

Lyue, *sb.* life; on lyue = in life, alive, 707.

Mallen, *pr. pl.* beat, 508. Cf. Lat. *malleus,* E. *mallet.*

Manas, *sb.* a threat, threatening, 46. O.F. *manace,* Lat. *minatio.* See Melen.

Maumetes, *sb. pl.* idols, 102, 373. Ch.

Maystrie, *sb.* mastery, might, 398. Ch.

Medlen, *v.* to mingle, 507; *stoures to medlen* means "battles to be engaged in." See Struien.

Meeten, *pr. pl.* meet, 508.

Melen, *pr. pl.* speak; melen of manas = speak in a threatening manner, 46; 2 *p. s.* melest, 106; *pt. pl.* meleden, 130. Will. of P.

Mene, 2 *p. pl. pr.* ye say, speak, 379; *pr. s.* menes, speaks, 403. A.S. *mænan.* All. P.

Mensked, *pp.* worshipped, honoured, 146. All. P. and Will. of P.

Messager, *sb.* messenger, 324, 403. Ch.

Mette, *pt. s.* dreamed, 442. Ch.

Miȝtful, *adj.* mighty, 508.

Mooder, *sb.* mother, 98.

Morwe, *sb.* morning, 26, 473. Ch.

Moste, *adj. superl.* most, i. e. greatest, 375.

Mot, *pr. s.* must, shall, 701; *pl.* mote, 166; moten, 603; 2 *p. s.* most, 230.

Mowe, *pr. pl.* may, 602; *pt. pl.* mouȝten, might, 23.

Murili, *adv.* lit. merrily; *hence,* happily, joyfully, 255, 661.

Myle, *sb. pl.* miles, 417, 418.

Nare (*put for* ne are), are not, 338, 342.

Nas (*for* ne was), was not, 126, 146, 593.

Ne, *conj.* nor, 593.

Nedde (*for* ne hedde), had not, 118; *pl.* nedden, 247. Cf. Hedde.

Nede, *adv.* of necessity, 230. (We generally find the form *nedes.*)

Neodes, *pr. s. impers.* is needful (for thee), 163.

Newed, *pp.* renewed, 588.

Nis, is not ; nis not (= ne is not, a double negative), 66; nis (*singly*), 449.

Niȝt, (*used as a pl.*) nights, 6.

Nome, *sb.* name, 10, 78, 156, 684, 694.

Nomelich, *adv.* namely, 670.

Nomen, *pp.* taken, 405. Ch.

No-skunus (*for* nos kunus = nones kunnes), of no kind ; for nos-kunus þinge = for a thing of no kind, i. e. on no account, 219. See the note.

Not (*for* ne wot), know not, 467. *Cf.* Nuste *and* Wite.

Note, *v.* to use, make good use of, 588. A.S. *notian.* "Notun or vsyn. *Utor.*" Prompt. Parv.

Nouþer, *adv.* not where, not whither ; nouþer þei nusten, (not) whither they knew not, 702.

Nouwe, *adv.* now, 1 ;—nou, 29.

Nouȝt, *sb.* nothing, i. e. of no value, of no avail, 379.

Nouȝwhere, *adv.* nowhere, 328, 357.

Nul (*for* ne wol), I will not, 249.

Nuste (*for* ne wuste), *pt. pl.* knew not, 129, 199, 608 ;—nusten, 702. *See* Wuste.

O, one, one and the same, 146, 182 ;—on, 200.

Of, *prep.* away from, out of, 385 ; *with a partitive sense*, some of, 404; for, 561.

Of-fouȝten, *pp.* wearied out with fighting, 552. Cf. For-fouȝten.

Of-scutered, *pp.* frightened out of one's wits, 71. Cf. E. *shudder*, G. *schaudern :* we have, in this poem, *fert* for *ferd*, *wynt* for *wynd*, and

bert for *berd ;* so here, *of-scutered* seems to be for *of-schudered.* But there seems to be no other instance of the word.

On, *adj.* one, 178 ; þat on = the one, 183, 261 ;—on = one and the same, 200 ;—on þe hiȝeste þing, a thing which is the most mysterious, 254.

On, *prep.; stremynge* on = streaming with, 560.

Onswere, *v.* to answer, 377 ; *pr. s.* onsweres, 393, 467; *pl. s.* on-swerde, 674.

Or, your, 65. So in P. Pl. A.

Oþer, *conj.* or, 201.

Oþer, *adj.* second ; þat oþer = the second, 262 ;—þe oþur, 271 ;—þat oþer = the other, 396.

Ou. *See* Ow.

Ouer-charged, *pp.* oppressed, 552.

Oune, *adj.* own ; on or oune = in our own (land), i. e. while it is still ours ; *or* in our own (way) ; *or perhaps*, on behalf of our own, *or* alone, 495. The *precise* meaning seems uncertain.

Oure, your, 245, 373, 493. So in P. Pl. A.

Out, *sb.* aught, any whit, anything, 171, 369, 651 ; at all, in any way, 370 ;—ouȝt, 488.

Ouþer, *adj.* either, 184.

Out-wiþ, *adv.* without, on the outer side, outwardly, 186. Cf. Jamieson's Sc. Dict.

Ouȝt, *sb.* aught, 488. *See* Out.

Ouȝte, *pt. s.* possessed, 36, 425 ; —auȝte, 434 ; 2 *p.* euele ouȝtest, ill oughtest, i. e. oughtest not (to have done), 486. See *Out*, Will. of P.

Ow, you, *acc. of* ȝe, 67, 250 ; *dat.* ou, 73, 460 ; *acc.* ou, 461. So in P. Pl. A.

Oygnemens, *sb. pl.* ointments, 303.

Pallede, *pt. s.* he thrust down, knocked over, 499. P. Pl. B. xvi. 30, 51.

Parti, *sb.* a part, 45. Ch.

Payet, *pp.* pleased, satisfied, appeased, 350. Ch.

Pertly, *adv.* openly, clearly, 141. Will. of P.

Pleye him, *v. reflex.* to amuse himself, 458.

Pol-hache, *sb.* pole-axe, 499. Cf. Hache.

Pors, *sb.* lit. a purse; a bag in which offerings for the idols were kept, 387.

Prest, *adv.* quickly, 459. Cf. *Prestly*, Will. of P.

Preue, *v.* to prove, experience, 389; *pt. s.* preuede, proved, tested the strength of, 500. Ch.

Prikynge, *pres. part.* pricking, spurring, 459. Will. of P.

Proues, *imp. pl.* essay ye, test ye, 373. Cf. Preue.

Put, *sb.* pit, underground prison, 4, 221. A.S. *pytt*.

Rad, *adv.* quickly, 565;—radly, 629. Cf. *redeli* in l. 630. See *Redeli*, Will. of P.

Radde, *pt. s.* read, 643.

Red, *sb.* counsel, 63, 491. A.S. *ræd*.

Redi, *adj.* ready, convenient, 444.

Renne, *v.* to run, flow, 274. Ch.

Reowen, *pr. pl. subj.* they may rue, 491. Ch.

Res, *sb.* attack, 491. A.S. *rese*, *ræs*, violence, attack.

Reson, *sb.* story, relation, matter, 76; reason, 138.

Rewes, *pr. s.* pities, 154; *pr. pl. subj.* reowen, may rue, 491.

Riche, *sb.* kingdom, 307. Will. of P.

Rihtes, *pr. s.* arrays, sets in right order, 451, 490.

Rikenen, *v.* to rehearse, 76; 2 *p. s. pr.* rikenest, relatest, 138; *pt. s.* rikenede, rehearsed, said over (the Creed), 629.

Rikenyng, *sb.* explanation, 444.

Roche, *sb.* a rock, 522, 604. Ch.

Roises, *pr. s.* raises, 234. (Probably miswritten for *reises*.)

Ronkes, *sb. pl.* ranks, rows, 599.

Roode, *sb.* the cross, 258, 269. Ch.

Roume, *sb.* space, leisure (lit. room), 444. Ch.

Roumede, *pt. s.* made roomy, made void, 597.

Roungede, *pt. s.* champed, gnashed with his teeth, 361. Fr. *ronger*, to gnaw. "*Ronge*, to bite, gnaw. *West.*" Halliwell.

Sacren, *v.* to consecrate, 302; *pt. s.* sacrede, 300.

Sad, *adj.* settled, firmly fixed, 258. Will. of P.

Same, *adv.* together, 120. Will. of P.

Sarrest, *adj.* sorest, 620.

Sauh. See Seo.

Sauor, *sb.* a savour, scent, 658.

Sawes, *sb. pl.* sayings, predictions, 618. Ch.

Sayȝ. See Seo.

Scaþet, *pp.* scathed, injured, 61.

Schaft, *sb.* shaft (of a weapon), 510.

Schal, *pr. s.* (who) shall, 82; 2 *p.* schaltou (*for* schalt þou), 104; *pl.* schul, nu t they, 45; 1 *p. s. pt.* scholde, i. e. can, 83; *pt. s.* scholde, 107; = would, might, 637; = must, 463; 2 *p.* scholdest, 641.

Schalkene, *gen. pl.* of men, of warriors, 510. A.S. *scealc*. All. P.

Scharpe, *adj. pl. used as a sb.*, sharp things, i. e. swords or weapons, 513.

Scheld, *sb.* shield, 445, 559, 680 ; *pl.* scheldes, 508, 516. Ch.

Schendschupe, *sb.* disgrace, 496. Ch.

Schene, *adj. or adv.* bright *or* brightly, 510.

Scheuȝ, *imp. s.* shew, 587.

Schindringe, *sb.* a cutting, hacking, 513 ; schindringe of scharpe = the cutting of sharp (swords). Cf. G. *schinderei*, a flaying ; G. and D. *schinden*, to flay.

Schon, *sb. pl.* shoon, shoes, 423. Ch.

Schon, *pt. s.* shone, gleamed, 510. Ch.

Schone, *v.* to shun, draw aside, refuse battle, 496.

Seche, *v.* to seek, 15 ; to go, make (his) way, 528 ; henne seche = depart hence, 655. Will. of P.

Secmede, *pt. s. (impers.)* was seemly, was fitting, 115 ;—seemed, suited, became, 564 ; (*pers.*) semedc, appeared, 183.

Sege, *sb.* a seat, 292. F. *siége.*

Seih, Seiȝ, Seiȝen. *See* Seo.

Seiȝe, *v.* to say, 142, 631 ;—seyn, 70 ;—sei, 157 ;—seic, 161 ;—seye, 199 ;—sigge, 200 ; 1 *p. s. pr.* seiȝe, 309 ; 2 *p.* scist, 120 ;—siggest, 352 ; 3 *p.* seis, 105 ;—seiþ, 419 ;—sigges, 209 ; *pr. pl.* seiȝen, 3 ;—sein, 318 ; *pt. s.* seide, 21 ; 2 *p.* seidest, 224, 435.

Selk-werk, *sb.* silk-work, embroidery of silk, 427.

Selli, *adv.* wonderfully, very, excessively, 94. A.S. *séllice.* All. P.

Selue, *adj. pl.* same, very, 303.

Semblaunt, *sb.* semblance, appearance, 65. Ch.

Semely, *adv.* in a fitting manner, soberly, 636.

Sence, *sb.* incense, 290.

Sencers, *sb. pl.* censers, 289.

Sende, *pt. s.* sent, 77, 483 ; has sent, 460 (unless we should read *sendes :* but cf. 590).

Seo, *v.* to see, 167, 192, 352 ;—I-seo, 498 ; 1 *p. s. pr.* seo, 138 ; *pr. s.* seos, 258 ; *pt. s.* seiȝ, 58, 112 ;—seih, 181 ;—say, 274 ;—sayȝ, 152 ;—seȝe, 200 ;—sauh, 269 ; *pl.* seiȝen, 15, 90 ;—seȝen, 282.

Seruede, *pt. s.* deserved, 482 ; *pp.* serued, served, 526.

Serwe, *sb.* sorrow, 705.

Seten, *pt. pl.* sat, 432.

Seue, seven, 95, 574 ;—seuene, 541.

Seueþe, seventh, 577.

Seyne, *sb.* sign, token, 197. A.S. *segen*, a sign ; Dut. *sein*, a signal.

Sigge, Siggest. *See* Seiȝe.

Signede, *pt. s.* signified, 185.

Signefies, *pr. s.* means, 349 ;—signefyes, 627.

Siker, *adj.* lit. sure ; hence, safe and sound, 475 ; sure, secure, 605. Will. of P.

Siker, *adv.* verily, 705 ;—syker, 664.

Sikerli, *adv.* verily, assuredly, 541, 654 ;—sikerliche, 574.

Sikernesse, *sb.* security, 623. Ch.

Siþen, *adv.* since, 4 ; afterwards, 9, 12, 224, 568, 708.

Sitte, *v.* to suit, agree, 120 ; to prosper, 224 (we now use *stand* in this sense).

Skil, *sb.* reason, matter, 71. Ch.

Slauht, *sb.* slaughter, death, 266. A.S. *slœge*, Mœso-Goth. *slauhts.*

Sle, *v.* to slay, 94, 364 ; 2 *p. s. pt.* slouȝ, slewest, 433 ; *pt. pl.* slowen, slew, 605 ; *pp.* I-slawe, 96 ;—slayen, 541. In l. 517 *slen* = they slay ; but it is not clear whether *scheldes* or *þei* (understood) is the nominative.

Sonde, *sb.* message, 470 ; hence, appointment, ordinance, 323. Ch.

Sonenday, *sb.* Sunday, 1.

Sore, *sb.* trouble, 449. Will. of P.

Sore, *adv.* sorely, 487, 542. Will. of P.

Soþe, *sb.* truth, 523. *See* Forsoþe.

Souht, *pt. s.* sought; souht vp = rose up, sprang up, 181;—souȝte, went, 634 ; 2 *p.* souȝtes, wentest, madest thy way, 431 ; 1 *p. pl.* souhten, we went, 636 ; 3 *pl.* souȝten, made their way, advanced, 594. *See* Seche ; and cf. Gloss. to Will. of Palerne.

Sound[e], *sb.* preservation, assistance giving security, safety, 675. O. Fries. *sonde, sunde,* G. *gesundheit,* soundness, preservation.

Souwe, *v.* to sew, 427.

Space, *sb.* opportunity (lit. space), 580.

Spedes hem, *pr. s.* avails them, 148 ; *pp.* sped, despatched, i. e. baptized, 9.

Spedli, *adv.* speedily, 580. Will. of P.

Spekes, *pr. s.* speaks, 38 ; 2 *p. s. pt.* speke, 218 ; *pt. s.* speek, 343, 346; *imp. s.* spek, 401.

Spice, *sb.* species, kind, 193. Ch.

Sporn, *sb.* lit. a spurning, kick ; *but used to mean* a tumble, fall, 581. The French text shews that Seraphe's fall was "his own," because he swooned away, and by falling escaped the knife aimed at him. See note to l. 575.

Spreynden, *pt. pl.* they sprinkled, 314. Ch.

Sprong, *pt. s.* sprang, leapt about, grew excited, 343.

Spute, *v.* to dispute, 148. Halliwell.

Sputison, *sb.* disputation, 343.

Stad, *pp.* placed, stationed, 397.

Starf, *pt. s.* died ; *apparently,* starf aftur þe deþ = afterwards died the death, 514. A.S. *steorfan,* G. *sterben.* Ch.

Starte, *pt. s.* started, 544.

Stiken, *pp.* stuck, pierced, 273.

Stiward, *sb.* steward, 518, 601.

Stoffes, *pr. s.* lit. stuffs ; hence, draws together, rallies into a mass, 601.

Stor, *sb.* store, 456.

Stounde, *sb.* time, 644. Ch.

Stour, *sb.* battle, conflict, 518, 548 ; *pl.* stoures, 507. Ch.

Streiȝten, *pt. pl.* lit. stretched ; awei streiȝten = went straight away *or* went away at full stretch, 456 ; *pp.* streiht, stretched, 519 ;—strauȝt, 560; *pt. s.* streiȝte to = stretched out (his hand) to, 544. Will. of P.

Strok, *pt. s.* struck, 567 ; *pp.* striken, 519, 573, 679.

Struien, *v.* to destroy, 507 ; *to struien* is the gerund, and means *to be destroyed :* cf. our phrase, "he is *to blame*," which follows the A.S. idiom. Ch.

Stude, *sb.* place, 576 ; *pl.* studes, 634.

Studefast, *adj.* steadfast, 220.

Sturede, *pt. s.* stirred, 567.

Sturten, *pt. pl.* started, 363. Cf. Starte.

Summe, *pl. adj.* some (?), 30 ; to some, 349. In both passages, the construction is obscure.

Sunnes, *sb. pl.* sins, 223.

Suwen on him, *pr. pl.* follow him, 668. Ch.

Swelten, *v.* to die, 377. Ch.

Swengeden, *pt. pl.* swung, i. e. rushed, dashed, 529. A.S. *swingan,* to swing, dash. All. P. *See* Swyngede.

Sweuene, *sb.* a dream, 441. Ch.

Swiþe, *adv.* quickly, soon, 27, 161, 451, 571; excessively, 235. Will. of P.

Swoune, *sb.* swoon, 583; where we should perhaps read *a swoune* = in a swoon: at any rate, *a, in,* or *on* must be understood.

Swounynge, *sb.* a swooning, swoon, 543.

Swouȝninge, *pres. part.* swooning, 513.

Swyngede, *pt. s.* dashed, rushed, 576. *See* Swengeden.

Syker, *adv.* truly, verily, 664. *See* Sikerli.

Teeme, *sb.* theme, 149. P. Pl. B. iii. 95.

Teis, *sb. pl.* ties, fastenings, cords, 504. It seems to imply that there was some kind of cord or string bound round his hands so as to secure the axe from slipping. It is spelt *teȝen* in Laȝamon. ii. 457; " teien heom to-gadere mid guldene *teȝen*," tie them together with golden *ties.*

Teiȝ, *pt. s.* drew, i. e. went, 57; —tei, strained, tugged, exerted himself, 149; — towen, pulled, dragged, 374. A.S. *teón,* to pull, draw. We find in Laȝamon the infin. *teon* (to go, come, approach, follow, descend, return, turn, draw) with pt. s. *teih,* and pt. pl. *tuwen.* In the 2nd edition of All. P. *towen* is rightly explained *drawn.* Cf. mod. Eng. *tow, tug*

þat, that which, 129, 190, 200, 210;—þat þat, that which, 138.

þauȝ, *conj.* though, 46; — þeiȝ, 125.

þen, *conj.* than, 592, 596.

þenkes, *imp. pl.* 2 *p.* think ye; —þenkes on = think of, call to

mind, 493. To *think on* = *remember* is a common expression, to my own knowledge, in Shropshire.

þenne, *adv.* thence, away from that place, 25, 368; fro þenne, from thence, 418.

þer, *adv.* where, 13, 58, 599 ;— þere, 20; þer as = there where, 17.

þester, *adj.* dark, 160. In l. 235, þester bi-gon = it began to be dark ; but it is uncertain whether þester is here an adj. or a vb. It occurs in Laȝamon and the Ormulum.

þhouȝte, *pt. s.* it seemed (a wonder to them), 606 ;—þouȝte, 677, 687; *pr. s.* þinkeþ, it seems (to me), 6.

þinkeþ. *See* above.

þise, *pl. pron.* these, 21, 337 ;— þis, 29, 419 ; — þis oþere, these others, 686.

þo, those, they, 60.

þonderde, *pt. s.* it thundered, 235.

þonke, 1 *p. s. pr.* I thank, 5 ; *pr. pl.* þonken, 471.

þorwȝ, *prep.* through, 97, 104.

þouȝte. *See* þhouȝte.

þouȝtes, *sb. pl.* anxieties, 177. Cf. Mat. vi. 25 (A. V.).

þreo, *num.* three, 6, 140, 150, 177, 194; — þreo maner, three kinds of, 194.

þridde, *adj.* third, 180, 263. Ch.

þroly, *adv.* eagerly, impetuously, 91. Will. of P. and P. Pl. A. ix. 107.

þrowe, *sb.* time, period, 6.   Ch.

þurleden, *pt. pl.* thrilled through, pierced, 509. Ch.

Tides, *pr. s.* betides, 372 ;—tydes, 617. *See* Tyden.

Titli, *adv.* quickly, 575. Will. of P.

To-barst, *pt. s.* burst asunder, was

broken to pieces, 384 ; *pt. pl.* to-borsten, *act.* brake in twain, 509.

To-clouen, *pp.* cloven in twain, 516.

To-hurles, *pr. s.* hurls *or* dashes in twain, 533.

Toke, 2 *p. s. pt.* didst take, 438 ; *pt. pl.* token, 456.

Tornen, *v. act.* to convert, turn (to the right faith), 23 ;—turne, 59 ;—torne, 229 ; 1 *p. s. pr.* turne, 215 ; *pt. s. neut.* tornede, became a convert, 179 ; *pt. pl.* torneden, 304 ; —tornede, turned round, 454; *pt. s. transit.* tornde, changed, 684 ; *pp.* 1-tornd, converted, 216.

Towen. *See* Teiȝ.

Trayed, *pp.* betrayed, 102.

Trayse, *v.* to betray, deceive, 624. Ch.

Treos, *sb. pl.* trees, 191.

Trouwe, *imp. s.* trow thou, believe, 184 ; 1 *p. s. pr.* trouwe, 216 ; 2 *p.* trouwest, believest, 372 ;— trouwestou (*for* trouwest þou), 617.

Tulten, *pt. pl.* tilted over, fell, 100. See *Tylte,* All. P.

Twayles, *sb. pl.* towels, napkins, 285. See *Twaile* in Halliwell.

Twei, two, 708. Cf. Tweyne.

Tweyne, twain, two, 670. A.S. *twégen*.

Twies, *adv.* twice, 136, 520.

Tyden, *v.* to betide, happen, fall out, 392 ; *pr. s.* tides, befalls, 372 ; —tydes, 617.

Tymely, *adv.* early, betimes, 415.

Vche, *adj.* each, 256 ;—vche a, 613.

Vchon, each one, 339.

Verrei, *adj.* very, true, 341.

Verreyliche, *adv.* verily, 351 ;— verreili, 443.

Vestimens, *sb. pl.* vestments, 294, 301.

Vigore, *sb.* figure, viz. the cross on the shield, 448. See note.

Viole, *sb.* a vial, phial, 290.

Vmbe, *adv.* about, all round, 394, 658. [Possibly *vmbe-mong* is one word, but I know of no instance of it elsewhere.] A.S. *ymbe,* around.

Vn-castes, *pr. s.* casts or throws open, undoes, 477.

Vncoupes, *sb. pl.* wonders, unfamiliar events, 187.

Vndo, *v.* to explain, 141.

Vn-housed, *pt. pl.* dismantled, 455.

Vn-huled, *pp.* uncovered, 515. Cf. P. Pl. B. xiv. 252 (foot-note).

Vn-keuered, *pt. s.* uncovered, 559.

Vn-kuynde, *adj. pl.* unnatural, without natural love, 242.

Vnneþe, *adv.* scarcely ; vnneþe seuene = seven at most, 540. Ch.

Vnsauht, *pp.* unreconciled, unappeased, very angry, 64 ; at strife, 433. Laȝamon.

Vnsely, *adj.* unhappy, miserable, 704 ; cf. l. 705. Laȝamon. Ch.

Vp-haunset, *pp.* raised up, lifted up, 515. *See* Haunsen.

Vr, our, 143 ;—vre, 32, 164, 245. So in P. Pl. A.

Vsede, *pt. s.* used ; vsede of = made use of, 660.

Vuel, *sb.* evil, sore disease, 633 ; —euel, 644.

War, *adj.* aware, 530. Ch.

Warpes, *pr. s.* turns over, lifts up, 257. All. P.

Was, *put for* who was, 19, 38.

Wasscheles, *sb. pl.* pots for holy water, 288. See note.

Wawes, *pr. s.* wags, moves, removes, 52. A.S. *wágian*.

Wel, *adv.* well ; so wel weore
þei = they were so fortunate, 33 ;
—wel aboute = just about, 165 ;
—wel a two hundred, i. e. about
two hundred, 521 ;—wel of vr-self,
pleased with ourselves, happy, 659.

Welde, *pt. s.* wielded, managed,
drove about, 600.

Wem, *sb.* spot, stain, 86, 180.
Ch.

Wemmet, *pp.* injured, 542 ;—
wemmed, 678. *See* Wem.

Wende, *v.* to go ; *pr. pl.* wenden,
they wend, go, 29, 313; 2 *p. s. pr.*
wendes, goest, 420 ; *pr. s.* weendes,
53, 237 ;—wendes, 546 ; *pt. pl.* went-
en, 191. In l. 211 *wende* may be *pt.
s.* = went, entered ; or it may be
an error for *wonede*, dwelt, as
suggested by comparison with l.
180 ; yet see *won* in l. 333. *See*
Won.

Weore, *pr. s. subj.* he were, 122,
652 ; 2 *p. s. pr. indic.* (= wast), 428,
430, 437 ; 2 *p. s. pr. subj.* were,
428 ; *pr. pl.* weore, 25, 33.

Werdes, *sb. pl.* destinies, fates,
prophetical writings, 317. See
Wyrde in All. P. [But possibly
it is a mere error for *wordes* =
words.]

Werret, *pp.* warred, 60.

Whappede, *pt. s.* lapped, wrapped ;
whappede us vmbe = enclosed us
round, 658. "Lappyn or whappyn
yn cloþys, happyn to-gedyr, wrap
to-geder in clothes. *Involvo.*"
Prompt. Parv.

Whon, *adv.* when, 25, 31, 622.

Whucche, *sb.* a hutch, ark, large
wooden box, 39, 237 ;—wȝucche,
267, 281. "Hutche or whyche . . .
Cista, archa." Prompt. Parv. See
Way's note. A.S. *kwæcca.*

Whuche, *rel. pron.* which, 270,
608.

Wiht, *sb.* wight, man, person,
196, 197. See the note.

Wihtli, *adv.* quickly, nimbly, 461.

Wisse, *v.* to shew, point out,
make known, 32. Will. of. P.

Wite, *v.* to know, 443 ; 2 *p. s.
pr.* wostou (wost þou), knowest
thou, 420 ; *pr. s. subj.* may know,
465 ; *imp. s.* wite, 86 ; *pt. s.* wuste,
58, 677. Ch. *See* Wustest.

Witered, *pp.* informed, 466. All.
P.

Witerli, *adv.* openly, plainly,
confessedly, 154. Dan. *vitterlig*,
publicly known. Ch.

Wiþ-outen, *adv.* on the outside,
316.

Wiþ-saken, *pp.* withstood, con-
tradicted, 178. See Laȝamon, v.
ii. p. 118.

Wode-egge, *sb.* wood-edge, edge
of a forest, 475.

Wol, 1 *p. s. pr.* will, 621 ;—
wole, 624 ; 1 *p. s. pt.* wolde, 640 ;
pt. s. he desired, 115 ; 2 *p. pl.* wolde
ȝe, if ye would, 67.

Woldestou (*for* woldest þou), if
thou wouldst, 640.

Woltou (*for* wolt thou), 646.

Won, *pt. s.* (from infin. *winne*),
went, entered, 333. Cf. the Scotch
use of to *win*. See P. Pl. B. iv.
67.

Wonde, *v.* to hesitate from fear,
hesitate to speak, 399. Will. of P.

Wondet, *pp.* wounded, 542 ;—
woundet, 555.

Wonen, *v.* to dwell, 180 ; *pt. s.*
wonede, 56, 635 ; *pp.* woned, 315.
Ch.

Wonges, *sb. pl.* cheeks, 647. A.S.
wang, wong, cheek, jaw.

Wood, *adj.* mad, 367. Ch.

Worche, *v.* to work, 49. *See*
Wrouȝt.

Worþe, *pr. s. subj.* may (he) be, 146.

Wost, 2 *p. s. pr.* wottest, knowest,
330.

Wostou, (*for* wost þou), wottest
thou, knowest thou, 420.

Woxen, 2 *p. pl. pt.* did grow, became, 433 ; *pt. pl.* grew, 452.

Wrou3t, *pp.* constructed, 204 ; worked, toiled, 554 ; *pt. pl.* wrou3ten, wrought, did ; his red wrou3ten = wrought his counsel, acted by his advice, 491. *See* Worche.

Wustest, 2 *p. s. pt.* didst protect, 221 (see note) ; *pt. s.* wuste, knew, 58, 677. *See* Witen.

Wynt, *sb.* a wind, breeze, 658.

3af, *pt. s.* gave, 439.

3e, yea (used where mere *assent* is implied), 170, 621.

3eme, *v.* to take care of, 309 ; 2 *p. s. pr.* 3emes, 310. Ch.

3ernloker, *adv.* more eagerly, 593. Both the positive *3eornliche* and the comp. *3eorneluker* occur in the Ancren Riwle, pp. 98, 234.

3if, *conj.* if, 329, 484.

3itte, *adv.* yet, 63 ; still, 334.

3ong, *adj.* young, 437, 479, 593.

3onge, *v.* to gang, to go, 34 ; *pr. pl.* 3ongen, 313, 394.

3or, your, 673.

3ore, *in phr.* of 3ore, formerly, 317. A.S. *geara.*

3usterday, yesterday, 330.

INDEX OF NAMES OCCURRING IN THE ALLITERATIVE POEM.

ABRAHAMES, Abraham's, 56.

A-longines, the name of a castle, 407. See note.

Appollin, Apollo, 376 ;—Appolin, 383.

Aramathie, Arimathea, 156.

Argos, the name of a forest, 36. See note.

Augrippus, Agrippa's, 19.

Augustes cesar, 424.

Babiloyne, Babylon, 318, 354.

Betanye, Bethany, 29.

Brutayne, Britain, 232.

Carboye, the name of a castle, 416. See note.

Cleomadas, 692. [The knight whose arm was smitten off (678), and miraculously healed, 681.]

Daniel, 318.

Egipte, Egypt, 60, 98.

Eualak, king of Sarras, 214 ;— Eualac, 520, 548, 555, 570, 582, &c. ; baptized Mordreyns, 695 ; his steward slain, 518.

Fraunce, France, 426.

Gabriel (the archangel), the meaning of whose name is "the strength of God," 291.

Galaad, Galahad, 231.

Galile, Galilee, 77.

Heroudes, Herod, 93 ; *gen.* Heroudes, 19

Ierusalem, Jerusalem, 24.

Josaphe, son of Joseph of Arimathea, 169 ; is called by Christ, 251 ; sees a vision of the crucifixion, 269 ; is consecrated as bishop, 300 ; reproves Evelak, 347 ; makes a red cross on Evelak's shield, 445 ; leaves Sarras, 709.

GLOSSARY TO THE PROSE "LYFE OF JOSEPH,"

PRINTED BY WYNKYN DE WORDE.

[The reference 27/20 means p. 27, l. 20.]

ADUOCATES, *sb. pl.* defenders, supporters, 27/20.

Aferde, *adj.* afraid, 30/7.

Affrayed, *pp.* frightened, afraid, 29/31.

Agaynst, *prep.* in an opposite direction to; agaynst hym = to meet him, 29/19.

Applyed, *pt. pl. in phr.* applyed vnto londe = landed, 31/22. The Latin text has *applicnerunt.*

Assumpte, *pp.* taken up, 30/34.

Become, *in phr.* was become = had gone to, 28/21.

Cast, 2 *p. pl. pr.* consider, 28/1. *See* Kest.

Closed, *pt. pl.* enclosed, 28/4.

Comynalte, *sb.* community, 28/20.

Condygne, *adj.* condign, 32/14.

Consecrate, *pp.* consecrated, 31/11.

Consequently, *adv.* afterwards, 31/5.

Dure, *v.* to last, 31/21.

Dydayned, *pt. s.* disdained, 29/34.

Effecte, *sb.* meaning, 28/27 ; 29/11.

For by cause, for the reason that, 30/11 ; 31/34.

Fynably, *adv.* finally, 28/18.

Gaderyd, *pt. pl.* gathered, 28/11.

Heedes, *sb. pl.* chief men, 28/24.

Hole, *adj.* whole, 30/24.

Hystoryal, *adj.* history-writing, 27/7.

In-fere, *adv.* together, 28/14.

Inioyed, *pt. pl.* rejoiced, 28/20.

Instructe, *pp.* instructed, 30/28.

Interyd, *pt. s.* interred, 27/14 ; *pp.* 28/10.

Kest, *pt. pl.* contrived, imagined, devised, 27/17. *See* Cast.

Knowlege, 1 *p. pl. pr.* acknowledge, 28/32.

Lettest bury = didst cause to bo buried, 29/28 ; letest be buryed, 30/11.

Louers, *sb. pl.* friends, 27/19.

Lyuynge, *sb.* victuals, 31/34.

Ouerloked, *pp.* read over, 29/11. Cf. *Ouer-se* in the Verse "Lyfe."

INDEX OF NAMES IN THE PROSE "LYFE."

GLOSSARIAL INDEX TO THE VERSE "LYFE OF JOSEPH."

Floryssheth, *pr. s.* causes to flourish, 399.

Fortuned, *pt. pl.* came by chance, 133.

Fransy, *sb.* madness, 252 ;—frency, 445.

Habytakyll, *sb.* shrine, 243.

Halowed, *pt. s.* consecrated, 371 ; *pp.* 376.

Hawthornes, *sh.* (miraculous) hawthorn-trees, 385.

Hele, *sb.* health, 294.

Henge, *pt. s.* hung, 222. *See* Hyng.

Holde, *imp. s.* take hold of, 72.

Hole, *adj.* whole, hale, 280.

Hoseled, *pp.* supplied with the holy sacrament of the eucharist, 275. A.S. *húsel*, the eucharist.

Hony-combe, *sb.* honey comb, i. e. our Saviour, 417.

Hye me, *v.* make haste, 158.

Hyng, 2 *p. pt. pl.* (ye) did hang, 42. *See* Henge.

Iaundes, *sb.* jaundice, 447.

Infect, *pp.* infected, 330.

Iubylacyon, *sb.* joy, 403.

Iwys, *adv.* certainly, 39.

Kay, *sb.* key, 53.

Layd, 2 *p. s. pr.* didst lay, 421.

Layes, *sb. pl.* beliefs (lit. laws), 197.

Lepry, *sb.* leprosy, 46.

Louers, *sb. pl.* friends, 95.

Lyghtly, *adv.* readily, soon, 141.

Lyued, *pt. s.* believed, 197. Generally spelt *leue*, but the spelling *lyue* occurs in P. Plowman.

Meue, *v.* move, 323.

Megrymes, *sb. pl.* the megrims, 348. See *Megrim* in Wedgwood.

Mo, *adj.* more, 196.

Myddes, in, in the midst, 304.

Ouerse, *v.* to read over, 93.

Parde = Fr. *par Dieu*, 372.

Parentycle, *sb.* order, society (or *perhaps* the abode of a society), 402. Cf. Low Lat. *parentela*, a society, order; F. *parentele*, kindred.

Perysshed, *pp.* pierced, 13. See p. 31, l. 28.

Pockes, *sb. pl.* pocks, pox, 330. A.S. *poc*, a pustule.

Pocyon, *sb.* potion, 443.

Prest, *adj.* ready, 147. O.Fr. *prest*.

Processe, *sb.* record, narrative, 366.

Purpyls, *sb. pl.* purples, i. e. spots a livid red, which appear on the body in certain malignant diseases, 347.

Pyght, *pp.* placed, put, 106.

Pylles, *sb. pl.* pills, 443.

Quycke, *adj.* living, 221.

Recure, *v.* to recover, 328, 344.

Remeue, *v.* to remove, 40.

Resed, *pt. s.* raised, 47.

Resplendence, *sb.* splendour, 422.

Rode, *sb.* rood, i. e. crucifix, 217, 218.

Rote, *in phr.* herte rote, root or bottom of the heart, 27.

Rowt, *sb.* company, 192.

Rychesse, *sb.* richness, 175.

Ryme, *sb.* rime, 349. [Generally now misspelt *rhyme*.]

Sakering, *sb.* consecration, 375.

Sanctificate, *pp.* sanctified, 401.

Sease, *v.* to cease, 351.

Semetory, *sb.* cemetery, 379.

Sendony, *sb.* fine linen or cloth, 22, 31, 70. Gk. σινδών, a fine Indian cloth, muslin. The word is used in Mark xv. 46, "Joseph autem mercatus *sindonem*, et deponens eum involvit *sindone*," &c.

Sepulture, *sb.* sepulchre, 21, 67, 71, 421. [This is probably a wrong use of the word, as we find in the Prompt. Parv. "Sepulture, or beryynge. *Sepultura*."]

Short, *v.* to shorten, 351.

Shyt, *v.* shut, close up, 375.

Sought, *pt. s.* repaired, gone, 253.

Spere, *sb.* sphere, 428.

Stere, *v.* to stir, 309.

Styltes, *sb. pl.* stilts, crutches, 335.

Syth, *adv.* since, afterwards, 241.

Thaungell = the angel, 206.

Unclapsed, *pp.* unclasped, opened, 7.

Vykary, *sb.* vicar, 253.

Walnot tree (a miraculous one), 378.

Wende, *v.* to go, return, 73.

Werne, *v.* to oppose, 164. See Gl. to W. of Palerne.

Whether, *adv.* whither, 263.

Wo, *adj.* (?) sorrowful (?) 94. [I think it would be better grammar to read *theym was wo* = it was woe to them.]

Wrestes, *pt. s.* screws, twists, forces, 388. The *wrest* is a turn-screw for tuning up instruments.

INDEX OF NAMES IN THE VERSE "LYFE."

Abyngdon, John, 337.

Alys, i. e. Alice, 329.

Anna, i. e. Annas, 53.

Aramathye, 238;—Aromathy, 14, 24;—Armathya, 89.

Aueragas = Arviragus, 194.

Auilonye, 198.

Banwell, 258.

Barnabe, St (June 11), 382.

Benet, Walter, 329.

Browne, Robert, 297.

Brytayne, 114, 193.

Cayphas, 53;—Cayphace, 82.

Comtone, 313.

Dauyd, St, 370, 372.

Doltyng, 235.

Englande, 113.

Ester euen = Easter eve, 135.

Fraunce, 118.

Gabryell, 206.

Glastenbury, 199, 212, 228, 231, 240.

Gyldon, John, 305.

Henry (the Seventh), 234.

Iewes, 33;—Iues, 49.

Ilchester, 282;—Ylchester, 298.

Iosephas, the son of Joseph, 121, 195